ABOUT SUFFOLK

ABOUT SUFFOLK

*An anthology
compiled and edited by
Mike Reynolds*

Illustrated by Martin Knowelden

THE BOYDELL PRESS · IPSWICH

Introduction and selection © Mike Reynolds 1978

First published 1978 by
The Boydell Press Ltd.,
P.O. Box 24,
Ipswich IP1 1JJ

British Library Cataloguing in Publication Data

About Suffolk.
   1. Suffolk – History – Addresses, essays, lectures
   I. Reynolds, Mike
   942.6′4′008   DA670.S9

   ISBN 0–85115–093–4

Printed in Great Britain by
Fletcher & Son Ltd, Norwich

Contents

About Suffolk

My ideal anthology would have no introduction. The aim, after all, is so to choose the pieces that they form, in their new incarnation, a logical and coherent whole. Where the subject is a county the second aim is to cover it in all its aspects and at every stage of its development: to mix the prose with the poetry and the past with the present so that a picture – in depth – unfolds. Love of the subject is perhaps the other ingredient which makes a good anthology greater than the sum of its parts.

So the amount of explaining I have to do at the outset tells you, in a sense, how far short I have fallen of my own ideal. I shall try and keep the following brief remarks factual. The temptation of course is to use the time-honoured disarming phrases – "an unashamedly personal selection" is my favourite in this line. How can anyone criticise that?

I have called it *About Suffolk* to cover both senses of the term. My attempt has been to cover most of the ages and many of the moods in the history of a sturdy and beautiful county. Not that it is particularly beautiful in the spectacular sense – this book does not overflow with passages of the idyllic descriptive type. Rather it seems to me to be a county where there is a quiet harmony between man and the soil (despite all the years of struggle), where the ground is beautiful because it is worked and where remarkably little has changed, in comparison with other counties, over the time-scale covered on the following pages.

Suffolk today is not among the largest English counties (no. 13) and not the most densely populated. It is known for agriculture, its associated industries and tourism. The east of the county is now the more remote, unchanging area. Yet the Suffolk coast was once a seat of great wealth and pride – as Pevsner says, "the chain of churches which runs Lowestoft–Kessingland–Covehithe–Southwold–Walberswick–Blythburgh–Aldeburgh is unforgettable". Future historians may one day look back to a similar chain of nuclear power-stations cooled by the North Sea and powering 21st-century Britain.

Going far back, we should not be surprised that there was something special about the inhabitants of the tract of land bordered on one side by the North Sea and on the other by forest and the only main passage northwards, the Icknield Way. The early wealth of Suffolk – and its leading status by the 11th century – has been noted by many commentators. Its inhabitants did not appear quick to integrate with the rest of England, their energies taking them across the seas to all parts of Europe – items unearthed at Sutton Hoo have left no doubt of very early and extensive forays out of East Anglia. Wool provided a much later foundation for Suffolk's wealth, while industry, by and large, left it alone. "Suffolk has been in the happy condition of a county without a history," wrote the *Quarterly Review* in 1887. It is true that apart from the fate of the one-time Bishopric of Dunwich, there have been few momentous changes in the county, but its quiet transition over the centuries is none the less absorbing for that.

I should mention some of the criteria for the pieces selected. The many thousands of books which deal with, or allude, to Suffolk fall into recognisable categories. There are those by outsiders who have commented on Suffolk with the stranger's eye – many of these are included. There are those born in the county who moved away and provided their own retrospective judgement – they too are to be found. And there are those who have just touched on Suffolk, for a variety of reasons, whom I have often found complementing an existing body of thought. Of equal importance are those many authors who have not been included. By and large I have not taken passages from that largish group, whose books are widely known and read, and who could be termed the professional writers about the county this century. Nor have I included passages from one or two standard works on the county and its possessions – Munro Cautley on the churches and their treasures, Pevsner on Suffolk architecture. My reasoning has been that it is a better use of the space available to point the reader away from the main roads wherever possible: but I have overruled myself in certain cases where it seems to me that a recent book says perfectly what I should have had to use four or five extracts to indicate as well.

I have left spelling and punctuation as I have found them in the original sources, except for obvious misprints, and despite the occasional aberration and inconsistency. I have indicated thus . . . wherever a passage has been shortened.

There have been two previous extensive anthologies of this type, to the best of my knowledge. *The Suffolk Garland*, or *East Country Minstrel*, was published at Ipswich in 1818. Its compiler, not acknowledged on the front cover, was the Reverend James Ford of Navestock. Forty-two years later, in 1860, that indefatigable researcher into Suffolk matters, John Glyde Junior, compiled *The New Suffolk Garland* (an abridged version of which is again available today). Both are fascinating, but now make heavy reading, the earlier volume for its remorseless emphasis on uplifting poetic stanzas on local themes; the latter for its store of personal anecdotes about local figures of little significance today. Glyde also published an account of his sociological researches in Suffolk (*Suffolk in the Nineteenth Century*) which has some passages similar in quality to the work of Henry Mayhew, although it lacks the consistent objectivity of the latter.

This century has seen one Suffolk anthology of a different type, the Earl of Cranbrook's *Parnassian Molehill*. The linking factor in his admirably wide-ranging compilation of poems was the eligibility of his chosen authors for the county's association football team. Apart from these three works, I know of no other pure Suffolk anthologies.

One of the apter titles I encountered in my researches was *The Two Counties of Suffolk*. East and West Suffolk are indeed very different, as I hope comes out in the text. I have tried not to concentrate on one at the expense of the other.

Lastly, to do my research I had to get up and go about Suffolk. What a lovely county it is! I encountered on the way a great deal of help and courtesy, and should record my thanks to all who assisted me in my research: in particular to Mr. Scrivener, the librarian at Woodbridge (which houses the Seckford Collection) who proved immensely patient and helpful to someone who wanted to disturb nearly all his books.

Witnesham, November 1977

AN APPROACH

The history of Suffolk, presumably from its lying somewhat off the beaten track, presents but few facts deserving of special mention. . . .

Entry in Chambers' Encyclopaedia

> *Thus by himself compelled to live each day,*
> *To wait for certain hours the tide's delay;*
> *At the same times the same dull views to see,*
> *The bounding marsh-bank and the blighted tree;*
> *The water only, when the tides were high,*
> *When low, the mud half covered and half dry;*
> *The sun-burnt tar that blisters on the planks,*
> *And bank-side stakes in their uneven ranks;*
> *Heaps of entangled weeds that slowly float,*
> *As the tide rolls by the impeded boat.*

George Crabbe, From Letter XXII, 'Peter Grimes', in *The Borough* (1810)

THE NAME

Where diversity of Authours do all concurre for signification of the name of Suffolk it were vanity well reproveable to bee curious in Etimologising; lett it therefore suffice to understand that so soon as ever the inhabitants of this land were reduced into any regular destinction, the county received the name of Suffolk, and such as here dwelled were by the Saxons (then lords over all) termed the people in the South, as scituated southward from the county of Norffolk, since which time it hath evermore reteyned that name.

Richard Ryece, The Breviary of Suffolk

Suffolk hath Norfolk on the north, divided with the rivers of Little Ouse and Waveney, Cambridgeshire on the west, the German ocean on the east, and Essex, parted with the river Stour, on the south thereof. From east to west it stretcheth forty-five miles, though the general breadth be but twenty, saving by the sea-side where it runneth out more by the advantage of a corner. The air thereof generally is sweet, and by the best physicians esteemed the best in England, often prescribing the receipt thereof to the consumptionish patients. I say generally sweet, there being a small parcel nigh the sea-side not so excellent, which may seem left there by Nature, on purpose to advance the purity of the rest.

Thomas Fuller, *The Worthies of England*

On a clear day – and they are mostly clear days in this part of the world – you can see as far as you can bear to see, and sometimes farther. It is a suitable climate for a little arable kingdom where flints are the jewels and where existence is sharp-edged.

Ronald Blythe, from the introduction to *Akenfield: Portrait of an English Village*

I. THE PAST

1. FORMATION

Geologically, Norfolk and Suffolk are the most youthful parts of England, the strata being among the last laid down, and not subjected to the great disturbances which have tilted, contorted and consolidated the beds in other parts of the country. The older deposits have little effect on the scenery, of which the greater part may be said to have the chalk as a foundation, while much of the subsequent carving is due to glacial action. Despite the long rolling undulations of the chalk hills, the gravel ridges, and the occasional escarpments, the two counties are essentially a plain, through which rivers meander somewhat sluggishly at the bottom of gently-sloping valleys.

W. G. Clarke, *Norfolk and Suffolk*

2. THE SOIL

The earth, or soil, which is of divers kinds, yet all of them very fertile. The Eastern parts of it, which are called Low Suffolk, and extends from the seashore about six miles into the county, are hilly, sandy and bleak, yet being tilled, produce plenty of rye, pease, branke and hemp. It is upon these lands that the Suffolk farms and graziers sow their turnips, chiefly whereby such great numbers of sheep and oxen are fatted for London, and other markets. High Suffolk contains all the rest of the county which for the most part being a compound of clay and marl, is indeed something dirty, but very fruitful of all sorts of grain, especially in the parts about S. Edmundsbury; but being level and woody, is chiefly employed in pasturage for dairies, in which the husbandry of this county excels.

Thomas Cox, *Magna Britannia* (1721)

3. SUFFOLK CLAY

There is not, perhaps, a county in the kingdom which contains a greater diversity of soil, or more clearly discriminated. A strong loam, on a clay-marl bottom, predominates through the greatest part of the county . . . extending from the south-western extremity of Wratting Park, to North Cove, near Beccles. Its northern boundary stretches from Dalham, by Barrow, Little Saxham, near Bury, Rougham, Pakenham, Ixworth, Honington, Knattishal, and then in a line, near the river which parts

Norfolk and Suffolk, to Beccles and North Cove; but everywhere leaving a slope and vale of rich friable loam adjoining the river, of various breadths. It then turns southward by Wrentham, Wangford, Blithford, Holton, Bramfield, Yoxford, Saxmundham, Campsey Ash, Woodbridge, Culpho, Bramford, Hadleigh; and following the high lands on the west side of the Bret, to the Stour, is bounded by the latter river, with everywhere a very rich tract of slope and vale from thence to its source. Such is the strong land district of Suffolk taken in the mass; but it is not to be supposed that it takes in so large an extent without any variation; a rule, to which I know few exceptions is that wherever there are rivers in it, the slopes hanging to the vales through which they run, and the bottoms themselves, are of a superior quality, in general composed of rich friable loams: and this holds even with many very inconsiderable streams which fall into the larger rivers. The chief part of this district would in common conversation be called clay, but improperly. . . .

Of that district I must observe, that my arrangement will startle many persons, who speak of *clay* in a loose and indefinite manner. I was told of large tracts of clay near Pakefield and Dunwich, and particularly on the farm of Westwood Lodge; but when I examined them I could not find a single acre: I found rich loamy firm sand worth 20s an acre, but nothing that deserved even the epithet *strong*. I was assured that there was little or no sand in Colness hundred, where I saw hundreds of acres of buck-wheat stubbles. All these expressions result from the common ideas of soils being not sufficiently discriminated. Land of 15s or 20s an acre, in the eastern part of the county, is never called sand, though deserving the epithet as much as inferior ones. The error has partly arisen from the title of *sandling* being given peculiarly to the country south of the line of Woodbridge and Orford, where a large extent of poor, and even blowing sands is found; but speaking with an attention to the real quality of the soil, and not at all regarding the rent, the whole of the maritime district may be termed sandy; towards the north, much inclining, in various parts, to loamy sands, and in others to sandy loams; but so broken, divided and mixed with undoubted sands, that one term must be applied in a general view to the whole. This district I take to be one of the best cultivated in England, not exempt from faults and deficiencies, but having many features of unquestionably good management. It is also a most profitable one to farm in; and there are few districts in the county, if any, abounding with wealthier farmers, nor any that contain a greater proportion of occupying proprietors, possessing from one hundred to three and four hundred pounds a year.

Arthur Young, *General View of the Agriculture of the County of Suffolk*

4. The Discommodities of the Soyle

Whereas it is said, being so seated as this country is nere the hart of the Realme, peopled as it is in the fatt of the land, which is a sufficient cause for the encrease of great wealth, if trouble some times of domesticall insurrections, or civil devisions, should betide, it cannott bee butt that it should bee sooner desired, quicklyer spoyled, rifled and overcome than any other remoter place should bee.

Richard Ryece, *The Breviary of Suffolk*

5. Early Development

The detailed estimate made by Sir Henry Ellis of the population of Suffolk as recorded in the Domesday survey reaches the total of 20,491. (Ellis, Introduction to Domesday, 488–93.) Taking this total and the number of churches in round figures, the result is reached that Suffolk possessed a church for every 50 inhabitants before the close of the Conqueror's reign. There can be little doubt that Suffolk was then ahead of all other parts of England – possibly even of Christendom itself – and it is equally certain that the result was in no small measure due to the earnest labours of the monks of St. Edmund and St. Etheldreda, who in their respective liberties and outlying manors had immediate influence over more then two-thirds of the county's area.

Victoria History of the County of Suffolk

6. Early Wealth

Suffolk grew wealthy early. The natural resources were these: her closeness to the mainland of Europe and to the capital city of the realm, combined with her peculiar population and productive soil. The easterly position meant first that the land was entered and colonised by migrant farmers from across the sea in the Low Countries and the Baltic, and then – indeed almost simultaneously – was all ready to take part in trade with those not entirely foreign parts. The Sutton Hoo ship-burial gave proof of very wide intercourse: "Frankish, Scandinavian, central European, Byzantine and beyond." (British Museum, 1947: *The Sutton Hoo Ship Burial: a provisional Guide.*) An extremely early English coin has been thought to bear the name of Raedwald's successor, Eorpwald (?625–?632). In their generation, Bury acquired a minster church and by *c.* 700 Ipswich was taking shape. The landscape was being conquered by an active and unusually 'free' people, whose medieval customs, especially of landholding and inheritance, have close affinities with those of medieval Friesland (the seven *seelande* that formed the coastal strip between the Scheldt and the Weser). This is not surprising, but G. C. Homans' comparative study is not widely enough known. For 'Dutch' influence in the Suffolk landscape is certainly not confined to buildings with stepped or curving gables.

Recovered after the Danish conquest, Ipswich, Bury and Sudbury assumed the form of *burhs*, towns with a ditch or other water-barrier that the whole township could defend against outsiders. The Norman idea was different. They at once started to build castles, primarily for their own family's defence within so many alien and 'free' communities. Then they produced Domesday Book, which gives an incomparable account of these communities.

Account-books are not everyone's favourite reading, and the English called this one 'the day of judgement'. It showed that Suffolk was the most thickly populated county in England, with as many people as Devon, where there was nearly twice as much land. In Suffolk only 909 slaves were recorded: invaluable to a colonising society, but a liability once it is stabilised. A more notable figure is that of the recorded freemen. With no less than 7460, Suffolk had well over half the total recorded for the rest of England. Here is the measure of Suffolk's economic and social lead, a main ingredient in her physical difference.

Norman Scarfe, *The Suffolk Landscape*

II. SUFFOLK HISTORY AND SUFFOLK PEOPLE

1. Its Character

Of the many autumn visitors to the county, which rejoices in the sobriquet of 'silly Suffolk', few perhaps think of it save as the home of pheasants and partridges innumerable: and it is true that its warmest admirers can claim for it nothing by way of scenery beyond the quiet home beauty which Gainsborough and Constable delighted to paint. It possesses, however, a peculiar character of its own. Cut off as East Anglia has always been, more or less, from the rest of the kingdom, its inhabitants to this day look down upon 'the shires' as a foreign and very inferior country. Many old customs still survive there, and much of the peculiar dialect which schools and School Boards are rapidly driving out, to the sorrow of philologists and antiquarians. Still, in harvest time, the labourers will come up and ask for a 'largess'; a girl is still called a 'mawther' and a snail a 'dodman'. If you ask a cottager how she is, the answer will either be that 'she fare wunnerful sadly' or 'she fare good tidily' – each sentence ending on a high note which makes the 'native' or home of the speaker perfectly unmistakable, even if encountered in a distant county. If you ask after her little boy, 'he is minding the dicky' (*anglice,* donkey); if you talk of the crops, you are informed that 'there's a rare sight o'roots t'ycar.' The words 'cover' and 'covey' are employed by a Suffolk keeper in exactly the reverse sense of that usually ascribed to them, while still stranger perversions of language occur in the use of the words 'lobster' for 'stoat' and 'screech owl' for 'stone plover'. The people are generally a clean, honest and industrious race, famous for making good servants, and chiefly employed in agriculture and fishing; there being, with the exception of Messrs. Garrett and Ransome's great agricultural implement manufactories at Leiston and Ipswich, but few manufactories of any kind.

Quarterly Review No 328 April 1887*

2. Attraction and Repulsion

Not only are the people shy, but the spirit of the country itself is independent, capricious and elusive – if you don't treat it properly it will, like an unresponsive tortoise, retire to the seclusion of its own shell and escape you for ever. That slight animosity of Suffolk attracts the right people and repels the wrong ones.

Julian Tennyson, *Suffolk Scene*

* Section IV of which devoted to an extensive article on Suffolk.

3. EARLY MENTION

Mr. Hopton of Blitheburg told me that there appere at a litle village caullid Wenhestun about half a mile above Blitheburg on the same side of the ripe that Blitheburg is on certen dikes and tokins wher sum great notable place. And sum devine that ther was sum great place of the kinges of the Easte Angles, and that ther about was the olde abbay that Bede spekith of in historie.

Sum say that the castelle and abbay that Bede spekith of was on the farther side of Blithe, wher a creke cummith yn a mile from Dunewiche, and about a mile and a half from Blitheburg at a place caullid . . . hille wher yet appere dichis and hilles, whereof one is notable: and this is more likely to be the place that Bede spekith of.

Mr. Sheffield told me that afore the old Erle of Oxford tyme, that cam yn with King Henry the vii, the Castelle of Hengham was yn much ruine, so that al the building that now ys there was yn a maner of this old Erls building, except the gate-house and the great dungeon-toure. . . .

Borow Castelle standith aboute the quarters of Laistofte yn Southfolk. (Burgh Castle, Lowestoft.) Great ruines of the waulles of this castelle yet appere.

John Leland, Itinerary

4. ELIZABETH I VISITS SUFFOLK

a) In the year 1578 the gentlemen of this county magnificently entertained Queen Elisabeth in her Progress, for tho' they had but small warning of her coming, they prepared so well for it, that at her entring into the county she was received by 200 young gentlemen clad in white velvet, and 300 of the graver sort in black, with fair chains about their necks, and 1500 serving-men on horseback, under the conduct of the High Sheriff, Sir William Spring. While Her Majesty remained here, she and her train were feasted nobly by Sir William Cordall, Master of the Rolls; Sir William Drury, near Bury; Sir Robert Germin the Sheriff, etc. And when Her Majesty left the county, wonderfully pleased with her entertainment, the Sheriff and all the gentlemen waited on Her Majesty to the confines of the County.

Thomas Cox, Magna Britannia

b) We may be sure that the Bettes family were among the throng who eagerly watched the dazzling pageant on its stately progress through Wortham to Redgrave, and from Redgrave to Brockford some seven miles distant. In it rode gallants in the rich costume of the day, their yard-long rapiers clattering against the gay trappings of their prancing steeds, and vying with each other as to the size of their dazzling white ruffs; following them, a host of handsomely clad mounted serving men, the silver badges of their various masters on their arms. Then the central figure of the procession, the Majesty of England, decked in the gorgeous raiment she loved sparkling with jewels, with her bevy of fair ladies, all in brave attire; the coaches in which they were seated 'putting both man and horse into amazement by their monstrous strangeness.'

Taylor, the water poet, one of "Gloriana's" loving subjects, describes Her Majesty's coach, generally drawn by six grey horses with tails and manes dyed bright orange, as a gaily decorated canopied vehicle sur-mounted by a huge bunch of plumes. It was, he strangely says, reputed by some to be a giant crab shell brought out of China, while others thought it one of the Pagan temples in which cannibals adored the devil!

Whether provisions for the Queen and her vast train were provided entirely by those whom she delighted to honour, or whether they were in part supplied by the royal purveyors, is an open question. Francis Bacon, younger son of Elizabeth's host at Redgrave, made a notable speech in Parliament some years later, pointing out the evils of the purveying system "No one knew," he said, "when he might not be visited with the unwelcome presence of these taxers instead of takers, or by whom he was despoiled, since they refused to exhibit their authority."

Miss Strickland tells a story of a farmer who, seeking redress from such unlawful exactions, placed himself in the Queen's way as she was taking her morning walk, crying out: "Which is the Queen?" "I am your Queen," answered Elizabeth graciously, "what would'st thou have with me?" "You!" cried the farmer, feigning amazement, "why you are one of the rarest women I ever saw; you can eat no more than our Madge, who is thought the properest lass in the parish, though short of you; but that Queen Elizabeth I look for, devours so many of my ducks and capons that I am not able to live."

"Suffolk," says Reyce, "groaned under the remedyless burden"; its annual contribution to the royal household in ordinary times being valued at £3616 of our present money.

Katherine F. Doughty, The Betts of Wortham in Suffolk

5. HARD TIMES – I

Sir, Your last letter to me was only a desire that I would name to you some bookseller of Ipswich to whom you might send some of your books, for the spreading the knowledge of it. Our men of that trade are so poor and have so small a vent for books, that I durst not do it; believing you would get nothing for them, and so I should seem to have betraied you into that loss. Whilest I was thus debateing the thing with myself the letter was worne up in my pockett, and never came to the file as is usual with me. So that I cannot send you either a coppy or the original now. My correspondence with you after that time was intermitted for want of a subject, and upon the uneasiness the money has brought upon me and the whole countrey.

I believe it is the same with you; yet rather than a blank paper I shall send you a narrative how it went with us in the east. In January last there was no silver to be had. All that passed was gold; so that I told my labourers I must pay them in guinees. No sooner was the clipped money cried down, but all the gold was drawn off and small clipped silver money became so plentifull and was thrust upon us so impudently, that no man knew what to do. The 4th of May and whole year's tax being paid in and passed, out comes another sort of money hoarded before, shillings of ninepence, sixpences of threepence, half crowns of about twenty pence apiece. These pass awhile till men, beginning to weigh them, found the defect; and, the king's receivers refusing them, they began to fall to their real value by weight.

Our justices of the peace, in our last sessions, threatned to prosecute all that weighed the silver money; and many were presented. Upon this, the small money stopped, and nobody would take it at any rate. The Londoners sent down the small money in good quantitys; but when it was returned to them would not receive one penny of it.

No trade is managed but by trust. Our tenants can pay no rent. Our corne factors can pay nothing for what they have had, and will trade no more. So that all is at a stand; and the people are discontented to the utmost. Many self-murders happen, in small families, for want; and all things look very black; and should the least accident put the mob in motion no man can tell where it would end.

Edmund Bohun, Letter of July 31st 1696 in *Autobiography**

* Edmund Bohun of Westhall Hall is an interesting study. "Bred a dissenter from the religion," which was established in the Church of England; he grew to be a royalist of royalists, a church-man of church-men. The Bohuns were an old family, but Edmund's fortune did not match his birth. An ambitious, honest, clever, contentious man; sometimes a magistrate delivering charges at quarter sessions; twice if not thrice, left out of the commission; a treasurer for maimed soldiers; a learned and rather voluminous author; licenser of the press; persecuted by political enemies; brought to the bar of the House of Commons; a friend, then not a friend of the non-juring Archbishop Sancroft who was born and died in the near parish of Fressingfield. His life passed in eventful times; and in 1699 he died, aged 56, "the upright and free spoken, but persecuted and unfortunate, Chief Justice" of South Carolina.

Henry Montagu Doughty, *Chronicles of Theberton*

6. HARD TIMES – II

John Thompson, writing from Suffolk, devoted the whole of his reply to the insurrectionary attitude which, he said, was developing there. "One of the most alarming symptoms of a decline is the situation of the labouring poor; numbers are out of employ, because their masters cannot pay them for work. What then is to be done? They cannot starve! They are sent to work in the roads, and are maintained by the poor-rate. Thus the evil day (payment) is postponed to some future time! I was informed last week, by two gentlemen who saw them, that they passed by a gravel pit where forty persons of this description should have been at work; on the contrary, some were ringing a peal on their shovels – some, acting as serjeants, drilling their men etc. Dreadful symptoms of a decline; and if some immediate relief cannot be obtained, I may conclude by saying:—On the verge, nay even in the gulph of bankruptcy."

A. J. Peacock, *Bread or Blood*

7. HARD TIMES AND PROTEST

It was during the second year of this present century, that I learnt of the bitter period of the hungry forties of the past century. It was due to the tradition that 'It's the poor that helps the poor' that sent me on an errand carrying a jug of hot tea to an old man who was sitting on a heap of large stones, breaking them into small pieces to fill up the pot holes on the parish road. Born in 1820, he worked hard for seventy-five years, having started work at the age of seven. Now living in semi-retirement, he was existing on three-and-sixpence parish relief plus half a stone of flour or bread, weekly. In exchange for this, he had to put in two days mending the road.

Whilst he was sipping his warm tea, he related what life was like in his youth, when most of his meals consisted of boiled turnips or cabbage soup. 'Gut fillers, they were', he said, 'with no body behind them.' Black bread, when it could be obtained, gave energy, because the flour with which it was made contained ground wheat, barley and horse beans. In those days he lived in Suffolk, where the people were known as Silly Suffolks. They were too! When the harvest came along, and gangs of Irish labour arrived, instead of electing a lord of the harvest, as they had done for ages, they found the day of sickle and flail were over; their place being taken by reaping machines and threshing tackles. It was the Irishmen who started to protest that these machines were taking bread out of men's mouths. Deeds followed words in an outbreak of smashing the machines. Gangs roamed the countryside during the nights, and farmers discovered in the morning that what was a valuable asset one day was, by the next, worthless scrap. Harvest operations came to an abrupt halt; came the period when the night sky was all aglow with burning fields of ripe corn. Dragoons were sent from Norwich to knock a bit of sense into Silly Suffolks' heads. Probably they did, but, being billeted in farm houses, it was only natural that the farmers' daughters and the serving maids, and even young farmers' wives, received a fair amount of military favours, in return for extra rations supplied by the soldiers. The Irishmen, the cause of it all, quickly left the scene, leaving the local farm workers with no money to buy food; nor employment to obtain some. Some young men, preferring dumplings to turnips, moved into Norfolk. Others enlisted in the army, having learnt by direct observation that women were aware that a red coat had more 'come hither' than a ploughman's smock.

W. H. Barrett and R. P. Garrod, *East Anglian Folklore and Other Tales*

8. Suffolk off the Beaten Track – I

Thence I passed by some woods and little villages of a few scattered houses, and generally the people here are able to give so bad a direction that passengers are at a loss what aime to take, they know scarce three mile from their home, and meete them where you will, enquire how farre to such a place, they mind not where they are then but tell you so farre which is the distance from their own houses to that place.

Celia Fiennes, *The Journeys of Celia Fiennes*

9. Suffolk off the Beaten Track – II

The 11th of this instant May, as I was travelling homeward from London into Norfolk, it was my chance to bait at an inn called 'The Pie' at Little Stoneham, in Suffolk, where I heard you and Sir Walter Raleigh much abused in words by one Andrew Baker and Merivale Martin, with others then in that house: who in open speeches gave out that it was reported to them by one James Parkhurst, of Aspulstoneham, that a proclamation was set up at Ipswich importing that you and Sir W. Raleigh were fled, and that they should be well rewarded that could bring word where you were. Whereupon I certified Mr. Chancellor, of Norwich, of these speeches, who came with me to the house to have examined the parties; and they denying the words, I caused them to be had before a Justice, one Mr. Tyrrell, who examined these two persons, and hath it in writing under their hands confessing the speeches, and thereupon hath bound them over to answer at the Sessions: whereat the host of the house is greatly grieved, and hath given me very hard speeches that I should betray any speeches that were spoken in his house.

Richard Tomson, Letter to Sir Robert Cecil, May 1600, Quoted in *East Anglian Miscellany* No 3900

10. A Suffolk Election

It is to be premised that the Candidates in this Election are three: Sir Nathaniel Barnardiston and Sir Philip Parker on the Puritan side; and Mr. Henry North, son of Sir Roger North, on the Court or Royalist side. Sir Roger is himself already elected, or about to be elected, for the borough of Eye; – and now Mr. Henry, heir-apparent, is ambitious to be Knight of the Shire. He, if he can, will oust one of the two Puritans, he cares little which, and it shall be tried on Monday.

To most readers these candidates are dark and inane, mere outlines of candidates: but Suffolk readers, in a certain dim way, recognise something of them. "The Parkers still continue in due brilliancy, in that shire: a fine old place, at Long Melford, near Bury: – but this Parker," says our Suffolk monitor (D. E. Davy of Ufford) "is of another family, the family of Lord Morley-and-Montcagle, otherwise not unknown in English history. The Barnardistons too," it would appear, "had a noble mansion in the east side of the county, though it was quite vanished now, and corn is growing on the site of it," and the family is somewhat eclipsed. The Norths are from Mildenhall, from Finborough, Laxfield; the whole world knows the North kindred, Lord Keeper Norths, Lord Guildford Norths, of which these Norths of ours are a junior twig. Six lines are devoted by Collins Dryasdust to our candidate Mr. Henry, of Mildenhall, and to our candidate's father and uncle; testifying indisputably that they lived, and that they died.

Let the reader look in the dim faces, Royalist and Puritan, of these respectable vanished gentlemen; let him fancy their old great houses, in this side of the county or that other, standing all young, firm, fresh-pargeted, and warm with breakfast-fire, on that "extreme windy morning", which have fallen into such a state of dimness now! Let the reader, we say, look about him in that old Ipswich; in that old vanished population: perhaps he may recognise a thing or two. There is the old "Market Cross" for one thing; "and old Grecian circular building, of considerable diameter; a dome raised on distinct pillars, so that you could go freely in and out between them; a figure of Justice on the top;" which the elderly men in Ipswich can still recollect, for it did not vanish till some thirty years ago. The "Corn Hill" again, being better rooted, has not vanished hitherto, but is still extant as a street and a hill; and the Townhall stands on one side of it.

Samuel Duncon, the Town Constable, shall speak first. "The Duncons were a leading family in the Corporation of Ipswich; Robert Duncon was patron of the" etc. etc. so it would appear; but this Samuel, Town Constable, must have been one of the more decayed branches, poor fellow! What most concerns us is, that he seems to do his constabling in a really judicious manner, with unspeakable reverence to the High Sherriff; that he expresses himself like a veracious person, and writes a remarkably distinct hand. We have sometimes, for light's sake, slightly modified Mr. Duncon's punctuation ... the questionable *italic letters in brackets* are evident interpolations; – omissible, if need be.

A SHORT AND TRUE RELATION OF THE CARRIAGE OF THE ELECTION OF THE KNIGHTS FOR THE COUNTIE OF SUFFOLKE AT IPSWICH, WHICH BEGANNE THERE UPON MONDAY MORNING, OCTOBER 19, THIS PRESENT YEAR 1640, AND ENDED UPON THE THURSDAY MORNING THEN NEXT ENSUING.

"The Under-Sherriffe having had order from the High Sherriffe of the same countie to provide honest and able men to take the poll, and to looke to get ready materials for the Election, went to Ipswich on Friday night; and the said High-Sherriffe was purposed to have gone thither the next day, but that hee understood the small-pox (nota bene) was exceeding spread in the said towne. Sir Nathaniel Barnardiston and Sir Philip Parker joined together and Henry North stood singlie, for the place of Knights of the Shire.

"The said High-Sherriffe came to Ipswich about eight of the clocke of the said Monday morning. (He lived at Stow Hall: he must have started early.) To whom Sir Roger North, father of the said Mr Henry North, and divers other gentlemen repairing, hee yielded to them to have the poll taken in a field neare the towne; and soe, after a little discourse without further stay, went to the Markett Crosse, and caused the King's Majestie's Writt to bee published; by which meanes the said Mr. North was carried about a good while before the other knights (Yes!) had notice that the said writt was published. And this the said High-Sherriffe did about an houre and halfe sooner than he was by law compelled to; that there might be noe just ground of cavill, as if he had delaied the business (Sir Simonds is himself known to be a Puritan; already elected, or about to be elected, for the town of Sudbury. So high stood Sudbury then; sunk now so low!)

"After the publication of which, the said High-Sherriffe withdrew himself to make haste into the said field (Mr Hambie's field; with the Conduit-head and big elms in it) to take the Poll. But before hee got thither, or any place was made readie for the clerkes to write, the said Mr North was brought into the field (triumphantly in his chair); and many of the gentrie as well as others that were of his partie pressed soe upon the place where the planks and boards were setting upp, as they could not be fastened or finished. All this time the other two knights knew yett nothing that the said poll was begunn in the said field; so as (so that) the said High-Sherriffe begann Mr. North's poll alone, and admitted a clerke. The said Sir Roger North proffered to write the names, with the clerke his (the High-Sherriff's) Under-Sherriffe had before appointed, which hee (the High-Sherriff) conceived hee was not in law bound unto.

"Having then taken the poll a while, in the said Sir Roger North's presence and his said sonne's, the companie did tread upon the said planks with such extreme violence, as having divers times borne them downe upon the said High-Sherriffe; and hee having used all meanes of entreatie and perswasion to desire them to beare off, as did the said Sir Roger North also, – the said High-Sherriffe was at the last forced to give over . . .

"The said High Sherriffe did there, without eating or drinking, assist the said Mr. North, from about nine of the clocke in the morning till it grew just upon night, notwithstanding it was in the open field, and a verie cold and windie day: and did in his owne person take much paines to dispatch the said Poll; which had been much better advanced, if such as came to the same had not treaded with such extreme violence one upon another. And whereas the said Sir Nathaniel Barnardiston came, about twelve of the clocke that forenoone, to the said High-Sherriffe, desiring him that all the companie might dissolve to goe to dinner, and that in respect of the great winde, the poll in the afternoone might be taken in the said towne of Ipswich (A very reasonable motion): The said High-Sherriffe, upon the said Mr. North's request to the contrarie, staide in the said field till the shutting upp of the said day, as is aforesaid.

Thomas Carlyle, 'An Election to the Long Parliament' (*ESSAYS*)

Carlyle's parenthetical reference to Sudbury is of interest: Dickens chose the same town for the scene of the Eatanswill election of The Pickwick Papers *and the extract below is also relevant.*

11. LAW AND ORDER

The organised rural police contrast very favourably with the constabulary employed in some of our boroughs, where it is notorious that the force is of very little use in the suppression of nuisances and crime. In Ipswich and Bury St. Edmund's, an efficient police force has been organised; but in the borough of Sudbury and Ballingdon, with a population, in 1851, of 6,043 persons, and a criminal tendency above the average of Suffolk towns, only *one* was employed. In the Eastern Division of Suffolk there is one rural policeman to every 1,965 persons; but in the town of Sudbury one policeman to 6,043 persons. This solitary Sudbury policeman, with a salary of 18s. a week, received notice of dismissal in 1854, it being intended that the Gaoler, who received £30 a year salary, should be paid £55 upon undertaking the additional duties of Police Officer. But, as the said Gaoler also held the offices of Town Surveyor, as well as Collector of Poor Rate, Paving and Lighting Rate, and Borough Rate, it may be readily judged in what degree he is capable of becoming an efficient policeman. The cry of "Economy" is raised as a cover for such imperfect services; but the fact appears to be that the proprietors and occupiers of public houses in Sudbury are an influential class. Many of them amassed considerable fortunes from the corrupt practices at elections, and a well-regulated police force would be especially distasteful to them.

John Glyde Junior, *Suffolk in the Nineteenth Century*

12. Suffolk Character

Those of my brother artists who remember the Academy twenty years ago will not have forgotten Samuel Strowger, the most symmetrical of models in the Life School, and the best of servants to the Institution. He was a Suffolk man, and had worked on a farm in Constable's neighbourhood, where he was distinguished in the country phrase as 'a beautiful plough-man', until he enlisted in the Life Guards, when his strict attention to his duties soon acquired for him the character of the best man in his regiment. The models of the Academy are generally selected from these fine troops; Sam was chosen, and the grace of his attitudes, his intelligence and steadiness, induced the Academy to procure his discharge, and to place him in the Institution as head porter and occasional model. Sam and Constable, who had known each other in Suffolk, were thus brought together again in London; and Strowger showed his readiness to patronise his old acquaintance, as far as lay in his power, by interceding, whe he could venture to do so, during the arrangements of the exhibitions, in behalf of his works. As they were generally views in Suffolk, they had peculiar charms in Sam's eyes, and he could vouch for the accuracy with which they represented all the operations of farming. He was captivated by one of them, a 'Corn Field with Reapers at work' and pointed out to the arranging committee its correctness, 'the *lord*', as the leading man among reapers and mowers is called in Suffolk, being in due advance of the rest. But with all his endeavours to serve his friend the picture was either rejected or not so well placed as he wished, and he consoled Constable, and at the same time apologised for the members of the committee, by saying, 'Our gentlemen are all great artists, sir, but they none of them know anything about the *lord*'.

C. R. Leslie, *Life of John Constable*

13. The Widow Edyth

The following, the third of 'Twelve merrie jestes of one called Edyth, the lyeing wydow, which still lyeth' is from a book printed by John Rastell in London in 1525, and relates an apparently true story of a Suffolk confidence trickster in the reign of Henry VIII.

> *This wydow then walked withouten feare*
> *Till that she came to Horrynger,*
> *Within two miles of St. Edmunds Bury;*
> *And there she abode full jocund and merrie*
> *For the space of six weekes and one day,*
> *And borrowed money there as she lay:*
> *Her old lyes she occupied still:*
> *The people gave credence to her, untill*
> *At Thetford she said her stuff lay,*
> *Which false was proued upon a day.*
> *Then one Master Lee committed her to ward,*
> *And little or nought she did it regard:*
> *On the sixth day after delivered she was*
> *And at her owne liberty to passe and repasse.*
>
> *Then straightway she took to Brandon-ferry,*
> *In all her life was she never so merrie;*
> *And there she borrowed of her hoste*
> *Thirteen shillings: with mickle boast*
> *Of her great substance which she sayd she had:*
> *To Bradfeilde straight her hoste she bade,*
> *Where she saide that she dwelled as than,*
> *And when she came thither, she fill'd him a can*
> *Full with good ale, and said he was welcome*
> *For his thirteene shillings; she had him burn*
> *And laughed tyght – no more could he haue –*
> *An oath he swore, so God him saue,*
> *The Justice should know of her deceipt;*
> *"A whore" (quod he) "heyt whore heyt"!*
> *The Justice name was Master Lee,*
> *He sent her to St. Edmunds Bury,*
> *And there in jail half a year*
> *She continued without good cheer: –*
> *But after she was delivered out*
> *Upon a day (withouten doubt*
> *My Lord Abbot commanded it should so be)*
> *When he was remembered of his charitie. –*
> *From thence she departed . . . (and to Colne she come.)*

Printed by John Rastell, London 1525

14. ABBOT SAMSON

So, then, the bells of St. Edmundsbury clang out one and all, and in church and chapel the organs go: Convent and Town, and all the west side of Suffolk, are in gala; knights, viscounts, weavers, spinners, the entire population, male and female, young and old, the very sockmen with their chubby infants, – out to have a holiday, and see the Lord Abbot arrive! And there is 'stripping barefoot' of the Lord Abbot at the gate, and solemn leading of him in to the High Altar and Shrine; with sudden 'silence of all the bells and organs' as we kneel in deep prayer there; and again with outburst of all the bells and organs, and loud *Te Deum* from the general human windpipe; and speeches by the leading viscount, and giving of the kiss of brotherhood; the whole wound-up with popular games, and dinner within doors of more than a thousand strong, *plus quam mille comedentibus in gaudio magno.*

In such manner is the selfsame Samson once again returning to us, welcomed on *this* occasion. He that went away with his frock-skirts looped over his arm, comes back riding high; suddenly made one of the dignitaries of this world.

Thomas Carlyle, *Past and Present*

15. THE ABBOT'S ROLE

After the return of King Richard to England, licences for tournaments were granted to knights. And a number gathered for this purpose between Thetford and Saint Edmunds. The Abbot forbade them, but they resisted his authority and fulfilled their desire. On another occasion fourscore young men, the sons of nobles, came with their followers to the same place fully armed for a return match. This accomplished, they came to this town to find lodging. But the Abbot, hearing this, gave orders that the gates should be barred and all of them shut in. The next day was the vigil of the Feast of St Peter and St Paul. So, when they had promised him that they would not go forth without his leave, they all ate with the Abbot that day; but after dinner, when the Abbot retired to his lodgings, they all arose and began to dance and sing, and sending into the town to fetch wine, they drank, and after that they yelled, robbing the Abbot and the whole Convent of their sleep, and doing everything they could to make a mockery of the Abbot; and they continued thus till evening and refused to obey the Abbot when he ordered them to desist. But when evening was come, they broke the gates of the town and forced their way out. But the Abbot solemnly excommunicated them all, by the advice of Hubert, Archbishop of Canterbury, who was then Justiciar. And many of them came to make amends, and begged for absolution.

Jocelin of Brakelond, Chronicle

16. The Love of the Individual

In 1879, the first of our really bad years, the floods were so high that many of the trees were killed, though some of them took a dozen years to die. Last year also we had a heavy flood in February, but it was of brief duration. Indeed the floods are neither so frequent nor so prolonged as they used to be, either because the millers below are more merciful in the matter of holding up the water with their sluice-gates, or because the bridge at Beccles has been widened, allowing the stream to escape quicker to the sea. Round Beccles itself, however, I believe that the water has been more out than usual, owing to the high tides, which dam up the mouth of the river. Never has such a time for high tides been known, and the gale of December last will long be remembered on the East coast for its terrible amount of damage. The sight close to a house which I possess at Kessingland, a place near Lowestoft, was something to remember, for here and at Pakefield the high cliff has been taken away by the thousand tons. In such a tide the fierce scour from the north licks the sand cliff and hollows it out till the clay stratum above it falls, and is washed into the ocean. Fortunately for me, my house is protected by a sea-wall, and though the water got behind the end of this, it did no further damage; but with property that was not so fortified the case was very different – it has gone in mouthfuls. Old residents on the coast declare that no such tide has been known within the present century, and it is to be hoped that there will not be another for the next century. But these phenomenal events have an unpleasant way of repeating themselves, and if this happens, the loss and desolation will be very great – greater even than that of the December gale.

For generations the sea has been encroaching on this coast. So long ago as the time of Queen Elizabeth it is said that three churches went over the cliff at Dunwich in a single Sunday afternoon, yet during all this time no concerted effort has been made for the common protection. If we were Dutchmen the matter would have been different, but here in rural England, unless they are obliged to it by Act of Parliament, it is almost impossible to oblige people to combine to win future profits or to ward off future dangers. It is chiefly for this reason that I do not believe that creameries and butter factories will be successfully established in our time – at any rate in this part of East Anglia – for to secure success I imagine that common effort and mutual support would be necessary, and to such things our farmers are not accustomed. Many of them, to all appearance, would prefer individual failure to the achievement of a corporate victory.

II. Rider Haggard, *A Farmer's Year*

III. SUFFOLK PEOPLE
AND THEIR LAND

1. EARLY RICHES

Lambert: *Peggy, the lovely flower of all towns,*
Suffolk's fair Helen and rich England's star,
Whose beauty, temper'd with her huswifery,
Makes England talk of merry Fressingfield!

Serlsby: *I cannot trick it up with poesies,*
Nor paint my passions with comparisons,
Nor tell a tale of Phoebus and his loves:
But this believe me, – Laxfield here is mine,
Of ancient rent seven hundred pounds a year,
And if thou canst but love a country squire,
I will enfeoff thee, Margaret, in all:
I cannot flatter; try me, if thou please.

Margaret: *Brave neighbouring squires, the stay of Suffolk's clime,*
A keeper's daughter is too base in gree
To match with men accounted of such worth:
But might I not displease, I would reply.

Lambert: *Say, Peggy, naught shall make us discontent.*

Margaret: *Then, gentles, note that love hath little stay,*
Nor can the flames that Venus sets on fire
Be kindled but by fancy's motion:
Then pardon, gentles, if a maid's reply
Be doubtful while I have debated with myself,
Who, or of whom, love shall constrain me like.

Serlsby: *Let it be me; and trust me Margaret,*
The meads environ'd with the silver streams,
Whose battling pastures fatten all my flocks,
Yielding forth fleeces stapled with such wool
As Lemnster cannot yield more finer stuff,
And forty kine with fair and burnish'd heads,
With sprouting dugs that paggle to the ground,
Shall serve thy dairy, if thou wed with me.

Lambert: *Let pass the country wealth, as flocks and kine,*
And lands that wave with Ceres' golden sheaves,
Filling my barns with plenty of the fields;
But Peggy, if thou wed thyself to me,
Thou shalt have garments of embroider'd silk,
Lawns, and rich net-works for thy head-attire:
Costly shall be thy fair habilments,
If thou wilt be but Lambert's loving wife.

Margaret: *Content you, gentles, you have proffer'd fair,*
And more than fits a country maid's degree:
But give me leave to counsel me a time,
For fancy blooms not at the first assault;
Give me but ten days' respite, and I will reply,
Which or to whom myself affectionates.

Robert Greene, *Friar Bacon and Friar Bungay*

2. THE LAND

Suffolk is classified as a corn county, that is, a county in which the acreage
under corn is two-thirds more than the acreage under permanent pasture.
Its agriculture consists almost entirely of corn growing, sheep breeding
and feeding, and winter grazing or feeding of cattle. The soil varies from
light gravel or sand on the east coast, to stiff clay in the centre of the
county, "High Suffolk" as it is called (where no one will own to living),
and some chalk on the western border. The four-course system of farming
is almost universally adopted, coupled with restrictions against the sale of
hay, straw and roots off the farm. Rents in 1880 ranged from 7s 6d an acre
for very light sandy soil, to 40s an acre for good mixed soil farms, and 42s
for best marsh grazing land. The cottages, as elsewhere, are fairly good on
the large estates, very bad in the "open" villages, where they are in the
hands of small proprietors.

Villages are, however, the exception rather than the rule in Suffolk, the
cottages being generally scattered about the parish.

Report on Suffolk Agriculture presented to her Majesty's Commissioners by
Mr. Druce, from *Quarterly Review* no 328, April 1887

3. USING THE LAND

They were pleasant holidays in the old country; but it did not heighten
my enjoyment of them, and of still later trips to the dear familiar haunts,
to observe how steadily the neighbourhood was losing its old prosperity
and picturesqueness. In those far-away days, I seldom went to
Framlingham without hearing that yet another modest estate had passed
from a small to a great landowner, or without seeing new signs of the
social revolution which had for years occasioned my parents many a fit of
dejection. Houses, that within my memory had been the picturesque
homes of gentlefolk, were seen by their neglected gardens to have become
the dwellings of mere tenant-farmers, too mean to care for flowers and
ornamental shrubs, or too poor to cultivate them at an avoidable expense

of a few pounds a year. In places where several small farms had been made into one large holding, one saw that the houses, which were no longer required by farmers, had been divided into tenements for farm-labourers. It was about this time that one of the stateliest old halls near Framlingham – a grand old red-brick structure that had been for genera-tions the Capital House of the Warners of Parham – was pulled down, so that no vestige but a workman's cottage was left of so interesting a residence.

Whatever good it may have done the country in other respects, the New Agriculture has done nothing to increase but much to diminish the picturesqueness of my native district. On discovering they were hurtful to the crops, by guarding them from breeze and sunshine, the New Agriculture lowered the height of the hedges, and had recourse to other measures for making the Woodland less woody. If the disfigurement of the country had resulted in the enrichment of the farmers, I would have pardoned the New Agriculture for making the parts about Framlingham so much less picturesque than they used to be. I do not say the New Agriculture did wrong in reducing the hedges. On the contrary, I believe it to have done right from the mere agriculturist's point of view. But, alas! ever since the New Agriculture cut down the fences, the tillers of the soil have steadily become poorer and yet poorer.

J. Cordy Jeaffreson, *A Book of Recollections*

Some would argue that the attraction of Suffolk lies in the fact that its land is indeed in use: Suffolk land is put to work and resists 'prettification'. The extracts in this section reveal various facets of the land's supreme importance and the effect this has had on those who live so close to it.

4. The Struggle

As a man I saw many such jungles in fields which had once grown good crops and which I had ridden over on a pony when a boy. That as I have said is the climax to which the heavy land over much of lowland Britain reverts if left to nature. I know a farm once, and now again, looked upon by some as 'the best farm in the parish' which by the end of the 1930's was in a fair way to returning to the state from which the occupier's Anglo-Saxon predecessors reclaimed it nearly 2000 years earlier. The farmer was hanging on by the skin of his teeth with about a tenth of the 250 acres still under the plough, to produce some oats, hay and kale for a few cows. The rest had tumbled down to grass, 30 or 40 acres of which had reverted to scrub and young trees, while save for some barbed wire round the few arable fields, there wasn't a stock-proof fence on the whole farm. Not being able to buy his own the farmer joisted other people's cattle for such summer grazing as the poor grassland provided, but those could wander at will from field to field and it took half a day to round them up. The hedges were so wide and so high that you couldn't see from one field if the cattle were in the next unless you went through a gap in the hedge or the broken gate to look. There were rabbits everywhere, on which the best and most conscientious of gamekeepers could make no impression, fouling the grass and eating the corn. The bushed fields and chain-wide thickets of thorns and briars which had once been hedges were impervious to everything save the bulldozer and gyrotillers which finally removed them during the war. Hidden away in them the rabbits were unassailable.

That of course is an exaggerated picture of the county as a whole but there were few parishes on the heavier land which didn't have a few 'bushed' fields somewhere or farms most of which had tumbled down to grass. Over much of Suffolk farms could be bought for £7 or £10 an acre, sometimes even less. On the light land and mixed soil barley and sugar beet could be made to pay and the best farmers on the heavy land, most of them relying largely on their cows, kept much of their land under the plough and well farmed. They had to be good and some were tough. There is the story of one man who had a gang of sugar beet hoers who worked like blacks from dawn to dusk: all had once been roundsmen on his milk round who had been 'careless' with the cash but the police had not been told – as yet. There was an unsolved murder in a distant parish: "I wish I knew who done it" he said, "I'd take him on." Well farmed or badly farmed, some of the niceties of farming had to go by the board if a man were to keep solvent and it was mainly the hedges which went. Riding to hounds one saw the worst, but even driving along the roads, where anybody's proper pride dresses the shop window a bit, the prevailing memory is one of high round hedges and occasional bushed fields for everyone to see.

The Earl of Cranbrook, 'The Suffolk Countryside', *A Tribute to Benjamin Britten on his 50th Birthday*

5. RURAL VIEW OF SUFFOLK

Health smiles around thy richly wooded dales
Luxuriant uplands, and refreshing vales;
Thy fields are like fairy garden, wide,
Where art and nature are so close allied,
Their happy union has subdued the wild:
Their home is here, and beauty is their child!

Fair district! where I drew my natal breath,
Awoke to life, and hope to sleep in death –
Where I have seen, and loved to see, green nooks,
Have heard, and joyed to hear, thy murmuring brooks –
Where I beheld, and gladdened to behold,
Lime, elm, ash, beech, and towering oaks of old –
Where I have felt sink in my heart the beams
Of the bright sun, that glowed on hills and streams;
Fain would I hope, in honour of my theme,
This dream of loveliness no fictious dream!

James Bird, printed in *The Suffolk Garland*

6. GLEANING

I must explain too about gleaning because in the old days that was an essential part of the harvest.

Very little gleaning was done here before the last war. It was practised extensively during the war because it provided food for the poultry kept by the cottagers; the poultry pecked the grains out of the ears, thereby doing away with the necessity of using a flail. Here are the customs regarding gleaning. No woman could glean in a field that was not in the parish in which she lived. No gleaning could be done until the farmer had carted all his shocks of corn and had got in the rakings. On this account, the careful farmer often left one shock in his field to keep the gleaners out until he was satisfied about the rakings. The gleaners lined up in the field just before eight o'clock in the morning. They were not allowed to begin work until the church bell rang, when with a cry of "All on, all on," they rushed to pick up the ears of corn. They continued until six in the afternoon when the church bell rang again and all work had to stop: then the cry was "All off, all off". If a woman picked up an ear of corn before the ringing of the church bell in the morning, the other women would compel her to throw it down again.

I have a field called Harts Ley, of which twenty acres are in Wickhambrook parish and two acres are in Depden parish, with no visible boundary mark between them; but everyone knew just where the boundary lay. Years ago gleaning was in progress in both parts of the field at the same time. Bustler Cook was there.

He told me: "I were a little old boy and I were herding pigs nearby at the time. I see one of them Depden women go over into Wickhambrook parish and pick up some ears of corn.' The Wickhambrook women rushed at her; she fled.

"She runned like a hare, she did, till she come to the hedge – that were a great old hedge – she stuck there a while and afore she could get through, them Wickhambrook women had well-nigh pulled the clothes off her back."

When the ears of corn had been picked up, they were taken to the cottage and threshed with a flail. From careful enquiries, we found that a good gleaner could glean two sacks of corn in the season. Thus a wife could earn the equivalent of a fortnight's wages of her husband, for the old standard of wages was that the man's weekly pay should be equal to the value of a sack of corn. The corn was then taken to the windmill; there were five windmills around here.

Justin and Edith Brooke, *Suffolk Prospect*

7. A DIFFERENT SORT OF GLEANING

Where did the labourer come in? It is here we touch a sore point, for it must be confessed that between him and the game preserver there was not much love lost; he was ill-paid, hard-worked, had lost his parish allowance under the new Poor Law, and was generally in a sullen state of discontent. In the preserved woods and plantations spring-guns and man-traps were set, notices to that effect being placed on the fences or walls. The poacher was not infrequently a desperate character, and the shooting of a keeper was an act by no means uncommon. I could mention three or four manors whereon bloodshed of this sort occurred. Among young men it was regarded as rather in the nature of 'a lark' to go out with cudgels for a free fight with the guardians of the night. I recall a desperate affray which took place at Campsey Ash, between nine on each side, being dismissed by the judge of the Assizes on the ground that it did not come under the night-poaching Act.

F. S. Corrance, Note furnished in the *Victoria County History of Suffolk*

8. THE SHADY SIDE OF SUFFOLK

> *Marauding gipseys, pilfering tinkers, sots,*
> *Who leave their wives and children for their* pots;
> *Trampers from Erin, begging through each place,*
> *If not relieved, abuse the Celtic race;*
> *Rick-burners, men too idle for the soil,*
> *And nothing hate so much as frugal toil;*
> *Incessant grumblers, yet, with means tho' blest,*
> *Will not enjoy nor give to others rest:*
> *Many, though inefficient, posts retain,*
> *Barter for health disease, and death for gain;*

Crude speculators broken by the rail,
Exchanging competition for a gaol;
Poachers ingrain, that dissipate their time,
And travel to the gibbet-haunts of crime.
Are these *good sons, good husbands, fathers? Such*
Contaminate the artless by a touch;
Some, uttering poison from their blacken'd hearts,
In the dread course of vice enact their parts:
Thousands there are – I draw a veil between,
And pity all behind the shadow'd scene!
May Reason guide them, Mercy change their ways,
Temperance *reform, and Virtue guard their days.*

J.R.P., from 'Fugitive Verses on Local Subjects', Ipswich library

9. THE LAND'S DEMANDS – I

"That's nothing to what you'll have to do," said Everard, wagging his finger at her, "when I've got all my herbs planted. You make very nice salads as it is; but then I'll show you how to make even better."

"How, Mr. Mulliver? I'm always ready to learn."

"Why, mainly by putting more things in." Everard was warming to this, his pet subject; it was the first time he had discussed it with her. "Young leaves of primrose, violet, hollyhock; sorrel, peeled borage-stalks and, let's see, rampion, burnet and purslane." He burst out laughing at the end of the enumeration.

"I believe you're using wicked words, Mr. Mulliver," she said, "or else you're laughing at me."

"I'm perfectly serious," he rejoined. "And then I've forgotten the seasoning; just a leaf or two, chopped up fine, of thyme, marjoram, sage, hyssop, fennel and tansy – only the tiniest scrap of that or it'll stink everything out   and marigold."

"No, don't forget the marigold," she mocked. "Where ever did you get all these new-fangled notions from, Mr. Mulliver?"

"They're not new-fangled, Mrs. Quainton," he protested. "They're as old as the hills; and the people who used them were your ancestors, though why all you country folk have forgotten them I can't think. It's strange too, Mrs. Quainton, how it was all the nastiest recipies that lasted longest, all the remedies, I mean – up till the last generation, anyhow. My father, who was born near Halesworth, could remember being dosed with yarrow tea for measles, and I expect you can too."

"No, I can't," said Mrs. Quainton. "How old is your father?" she added more gravely.

"Well, he'd be sixty-four now," replied Everard, "if he were alive."

"How old do you think I am?" she asked in a low voice, with a queer little pout.

Everard looked at her and then at the hearthrug, trying to calculate. That time he had found her weeping at the sink she had looked almost fifty; at other times, when she was pleased, as she had been this morning, there was a maiden of twenty in her eyes; at the moment her face bore a pensive, elderly cast. It was no use trying to strike an average between the two extremes; then he remembered Steve Quainton.

"Well, you're not more than forty," he said, trying to be generous.

She shook her head, a little sadly,

"I was thirty-four yesterday," she said.

"Why, one year older than I am," he cried, amazed; and then, dismayed at his mistake, "I was badly out, Mrs. Quainton. I'm so sorry. It's true that –"

She stopped his flow of apologies with a gesture of her hand.

"No," she said in a low voice. "I know I look more than my age, and no wonder. I've had a lot of trouble."

H. W. Freeman, *Down in the Valley*

10. THE LAND'S DEMANDS – II

A very large number of children are employed at farm labor in this county. Both sexes are sent to the fields early in life to add to the scanty income of the family. John Pearson Esq., of Framlingham, says: "Every person in the parish employ children in crow-keeping. I dare say at one time we had fifty or sixty children employed in crow-keeping." In Hartismere, Hoxne, Woodbridge, Plomesgate and Blything Unions, children are very generally employed.

Much depends on the size of the child and the necessities of the family as to the age at which *boys* are first employed, but as a proof of the tender age at which work is commenced in this county, we name that at Mildenhall the witness said, "In some places (in summer) they begin as early as six years of age." A gentleman at Wickhambrook observes, "At the age of seven and upwards they go bird-keeping and picking weeds off the land." Mr. Moore of Badley said, "Boys sometimes come at 2d a day; little things that can hardly walk come with their fathers," and Mr. Lane of Framlingham testified that children sometimes go to work at six years of age, they usually go at seven. In many districts, however, nine and ten years of age are the most common to commence work.

The kind of work in which they are engaged varies in different districts. They are generally engaged in weeding, corn-dropping, pulling turnips, crow-keeping and assist in stone-picking, and, except in cases of scrofolous children, injurious effects on the health or constitution of children are seldom observed. In some parts however, they are employed in carting, doing man's work instead of boy's, attending horses with heavy tumbrils, and their lives are thus frequently endangered. The danger there is in this employment is thus depicted by an eye-witness. "If you lived in the country, as I do, you would sometimes see a sight which would make your blood run cold, and yet it is so common a sight that we country people grow accustomed to it. You would see a great lumbering tumbril, weighing a ton or two, with wheels nearly six feet high, loaded with manure, drawn by a great Suffolk cart horse as big as an elephant, and conducted by a tiny thing of a boy who can hardly reach the horse's nose to take hold of the rein, and if he can, has neither strength nor weight to make such a huge monster feel, much less obey."

John Glyde Junior, Suffolk in the Nineteenth Century

11. The Land's Demands – III

A good insight into the out-door work and living is afforded by the following statement:—

'Hannah Winkup, servant to Mr. Catt, of Whitton I am 15 years old – was born at Sibton, near Yoxford. My father was a blacksmith, my mother had twelve children, and one of them was deaf and dumb; went out to work in the fields when I was 12 – keeping birds, sheep or cows; I frequently done boy's work – keeping sheep or cows is to prevent their getting into corn fields. I had 3d a day; worked Sunday as well, but my master used to give me a dinner on Sunday. Have gone stone-picking, hay-making, weeding and dropping. Earnt 5d a day at dropping; like hay-making best. Stone-picking is the hardest work I done – so much ligging; the stones have frequently to be brought from top to bottom of the field and it is very cold work. I worked from eight o'clock in the morning to six o'clock in the evening. Got my breakfast before I went; was allowed one hour for dinner, from twelve to one; had no more until I went home at six. I had bread and cheese for breakfast and cold coffee, no sugar – same for dinner, and very often the same for supper. At other times mother would boil a dumpling for us for supper, this was in stone-picking time, when we always come home very cold. We were so poor that sometimes I have had to go to bed without a supper; generally had a piece of meat on Sundays not butcher's meat, but pork. Have been in service three quarters of a year, my mistress is very kind to me; she lived in the same village I did; I have £2 10s a year wages, and Missus gave me clothes worth another pound.'

John Glyde Junior, Suffolk in the Nineteenth Century

12. THE WORK

Hark! where the sweeping scythe now rips along
Each sturdy mower, emulous and strong,
Whose writhing form meridian heat defies,
Bends o'er his work, and every sinew tries;
Prostrates the waving treasure at his feet,
But spares the rising clover, short and sweet,
Come Health! come Jollity! light-footed, come;
Here hold your revels, and make this your home
Each heart awaits and hails you as its own;
Each moisten'd brow, that scorns to wear a frown:
Th' unpeopled dwelling mourns its tenants stray'd;
E'en the domestic, laughing Dairy-Maid
Hies to the Field, the general toil to share.
Meanwhile the Farmer quits his elbow-chair,
His cool brick-floor, his pitcher and his ease,
And braves the sultry beams, and gladly sees
His gates thrown open, and his team abroad,
The ready group attendant on his word,
To turn the swarth, the quiv'ring load to rear,
Or ply the busy rake, the land to clear.

Robert Bloomfield, *The Farmer's Boy*

13. AND AFTER WORK

'Owd Kennick, he take no nonsense, like I tell you with the farmer. I recollect he take me to the first pub I ever been to. It were at this village o' Barnfield. It were one of the toughest villages along the coast at that time o' day; and there were one pub there, called the *Shepherd and His Dawg*, strange enough. It were the roughest place I ever was in. You'd go in there and they'd drink your beer! And just pick on one of 'em, and it were like a-tarning over a hive o' bees. It were a regular thing if there was a row there at that time o' day, some'un would tarn his mug upside down. That meant: "Who's for it? I'm ready for anybody." Another sign were to go outside and shout to whoever you had words with, and then throw your hat into the air. Kennick used to take me in there; but no one turned his mug up to Kennick or throw their hat into the air. They tell me he could use his hands right well when he were younger.

George Ewart Evans, 'The Rogue Shepherd': from *Acky*.

14. Industry and Suffolk Air

"Is there no remedy?" we ask, as we go out together [*to the miserable lot of the city textile worker.*]

"A very simple one. In the country – say in Suffolk, where we have a hand-weaving factory – food is cheaper and better; both food for the stomach and food for the lungs."

"The air is better, so less money, you think, would be spent in drink?"

"Undoubtedly. Fancy yourself stewed up in a stifling room all day; imagine the lassitude into which your whole frame would collapse after fourteen hours' mere inhalation of a stale, bad atmosphere – to say nothing of fourteen hours' hard work in addition; and consider what stern self-denial it would require to refrain from some stimulant – a glass of bad gin, perhaps – if you could get it. On the other hand, the fresh air which plays around country looms, exhilarates in itself, and is found to be a substitute for gin."

"I have also heard that the atmosphere of London is positively detrimental to the manufacture of silk. Is that so?"

"Why, sir," replies Mr. Broadelle, stopping short and speaking like a deeply-injured man, "two days' fog we had in December last was a dead loss to me of one hundred pounds. The blacks (London genuine particular) got into the white satins, despite the best precautions of the workpeople, and put them into an ugly, foxy, unsaleable half-mourning, sir. They would not even take a dye, decently. I had to send down, express, to our Suffolk branch to supply the deficiency; and the white satins, partly woven there on the same days, came up as white as driven snow."

Charles Dickens, 'Spitalfields', from *Household Words*

15. Suffolk's Pride . . .

> *But come, my county, let me build thy claim*
> *Upon a base of more enduring fame,*
> *That thou hast earn'd thyself by art and toil*
> *First honours in the culture of the soil*
> *That prime of occupations and the best,*
> *Ordain'd divinely and divinely blest,*
> *That peaceful life which Patriarchs employ'd,*
> *Which Kings have lov'd and more than Kings enjoy'd.*
> *Here, SUFFOLK, is thy theme for glory – here*
> *For honourable pride the lawful sphere.*
> *Then rest your fame, friends, on your faithful ploughs,*
> *For here the staff of life abundant grows,*
> *And blesses him that reaps and him that sows.*

Robert Hughman, extract from 'Suffolk'

16. . . . AND GLORY

When court gan frowne and strife in towne,
And lords and knights, saw heavie sights.
Then tooke I wife and led my life
in Suffolke soile.
There was I faine my selfe to traine
To learne too long the fermers song
For hope of pelfe, like worldly elfe
to moile and toile

As in this book, who list to looke,
Of husbandrie, and huswiferie,
There may he finde more of my minde,
concerning this:
To carke and care, and ever bare,
With losse and paine, to little gaine
All this to have, to cram sir knave
what life it is.

When wife could not, through sickness got,
More toile abide, so nigh Sea side
Then thought I best, from toile to rest,
and Ipswich trie:
A towne of price, like paradice
For quiet then, and honest men,
There was I glad, much friendship had,
a time to lie.

There left good wife this present life,
And there left I, house charges lie,
For glad was he, mought send for me,
good lucke so stood:
In Suffolke there, were everie where,
Even of the best, besides the rest,
That never did their friendship hid,
to doo me good.

O Suffolke thow, content thee now,
That hadst the praies in those same daies,
For Squiers and Knights, that well delights
good house to keepe . . .

Thomas Tusser, *The Life of Tusser* (1573)

17. SILLY SUFFOLK

Now she was full of the charms of Carbury and its neighbourhood. 'Yes, indeed,' said the bishop, 'I think Suffolk is a very nice county; and as we are only a mile or two from Norfolk, I'll say as much for Norfolk too. "It's an ill bird that fouls its own nest." '

'I like a county in which there is something left of county feeling,' said Lady Carbury. 'Staffordshire and Warwickshire, Cheshire and Lancashire have become great towns, and have lost all local distinctions.'

'We still keep our name and reputation,' said the bishop; 'Silly Suffolk!'

'But that was never deserved.'

'As much, perhaps, as other general epithets. I think we are sleepy people. We've got no coal, you see, and no iron. We have no beautiful scenery, like the lake country, – no rivers great for fishing, like Scotland, – no hunting grounds like the shires.'

'Partridges!' pleaded Lady Carbury, with pretty energy.

'Yes, we have partridges, fine churches, and the herring fishery. We shall do very well if too much is not expected of us. We can't increase and multiply as they do in the great cities.'

'I like this part of England so much the best for that very reason. What is the use of a crowded population?'

'The earth has to be peopled, Lady Carbury.'

'Oh, yes,' said her ladyship, with some little reverence added to her voice, feeling that the bishop was probably adverting to a divine arrangement. 'The world must be peopled; but for myself I like the country better than the town.'

'So do I,' said Roger; 'and I like Suffolk. The people are hearty, and radicalism is not quite so rampant as it is elsewhere. The poor people touch their hats, and the rich people think of the poor. There is something left among us of old English habits.'

'That is so nice,' said Lady Carbury.

'Something left of old English ignorance,' said the bishop. 'All the same I dare say we're improving, like the rest of the world. What beautiful flowers you have here, Mr. Carbury! At any rate, we can grow flowers in Suffolk.'

Anthony Trollope, *The Way We Live Now*

IV. THE PERSONAL VIEW

This is the largest section of this book, and could have been twice as long again: the theme is the effect of time spent in Suffolk on the individual. The writing is as varied in quality as the types of source material I have used, but the aim has been to give free rein to the individual voice, past and present.

1. A GLORIOUS COUNTY

Suffolk, the birthplace and inspiration of Constable and Gainsborough, the loveliest of English painters; the home of Crabbe, the most English of poets; Suffolk with its rolling, intimate countryside; its heavenly Gothic churches, big and small; its marshes, with those wild seabirds; its grand ports and its little fishing villages. I am firmly rooted in this glorious county. And I proved this to myself when I once tried to live somewhere else.

Benjamin Britten, Speech made in 1951 in Lowestoft, quoted in 'Benjamin Britten: His Life and Operas' by E. W. White

2. EVENING

But to understand Suffolk ways and to hear Suffolk talk it is necessary to linger in the villages and to gossip with the sons of the soil. The agricultural villages are only articulate in eventide, when they give themselves up to play and gossip. Then, as the long summer day draws to its close, the children find romance in the lengthening shadows, in which their games of robbers and pirates seem much more convincing than they could be made to appear in the glare of the midday sun; the farm labourers slouch off to their evening, over quarts of 'bellywengins' at the pub, and the coy mawthers find the twilight a seasonable time for nannicking with the hudderens. This, which may seen unmeaning gibberish to those unacquainted with the peculiar dialect of East Anglia, merely signifies the girls flirting with the 'other ones' – the young men, in short.

But a mawther may be of any age. A baby girl is a mawther, and so is a grandame. It is a curiosity of speech which is apt to startle the stranger who first hears it applied to a girl who has hardly yet learned to toddle, in the maternal threat, to be heard any day in any Suffolk village, "Yow come 'ere, mawther, this instant moment, or I'll spank yow, so I 'ool." "Yow" of course is the Essex, Suffolk and Norfolk shibboleth for "you", by which a native of these parts may be immediately distinguished anywhere.

55

When the labourers have trudged over to their "shants o' gatter" or quarts and pots of beer – the bellywengins or belly vengeance aforesaid; when the children have been put to bed, and the mawthers and the hudderens have gone nannicking off together in the gathering dusk, then is the gossiping time, both of the housewives and of the labourers.

Charles Harper, *The Norwich Road*

3. Master Charley – A Suffolk Labourer's Story

The Owd master at the Hall had two children – Mr. James and Miss Mary. Mr. James was ivver so much owder than Miss Mary. She come kind o' unexpected like, and she warn't but a little thing when she lost her mother. When she got owd enough Owd Master sent her to a young ladies skule. She was there a soot o' years, and when she come to stäa at home, she *was* such a pretty young lady, *that* she was. She was werry fond of cumpany, but there warn't the lissest bit wrong about her. There was a young gentleman, from the shêres, who lived at a farm in the next parish, where he was come to larn farmin'. He was werry fond of her, and though his own folks din't like it, it was all sattled that he was soon to marry her. Then he heard suffen about her, which warn't a bit true, and he went awäa, and was persuaded to marry somebody else. Miss Mary took on bad about it, but that warn't the wust of it. She had a baby before long, and he was the father on't.

O lawk, a lawk! how the owd Master did break out when he hear'd of it! My mother lived close by, and nussed poor Miss Mary, so I've h'ard all about it. He woun't let the child stop in the house, but sent it awäa to a house three miles off, where the woman had lost her child. But when Miss Mary got about, the woman used to bring the baby – he was "Master Charley" – to my mother's. One däa, when she went down, my mother told her that he warn't well; so off she went to see him. When she got home she was late, and the owd man was kep' waitin' for his dinner. As soon as he see her, he roared out, "What! hev yeou bin to see yar bastard?" "Oh father," says she, "yeou shoun't säa so." "Shoun't säa so," said he, "shoun't I? I can säa wuss than that.' And then he called her a bad name. She got up, nivver said a wâdd, but walked straight out of the front door. They din't take much notiz at fust, but when she din't come back, they got scared, and looked for her all about; and at last they found her in the môot, at the bottom of the orchard.

O lawk, a lawk!

The Owd Master nivver could howd up arter that. 'Fore that, if he was put out, yeou could hear 'im all over the farm, a-cussin' and swearin'. He werry seldom spôok to anybody now, but he was alluz about arly and late; nôthin' seemed to tire him. 'Fore that he nivver went to chârch; now he went reg'ler. But he wud säa sometimes, comin' out, "Parson's a fule." But if anybody was ill, he bod 'em go up to the Hall and ax for suffen. There was young Farmer Whoo's wife was werry bad, and the doctor säa that what she wanted was London poort. So he sent my father to the marchant at Ipswich, to bring back four dozen. Arter dark he was to lave it at the house, but not to knock. They nivver knew where ta come from till arter he died. But he fare to get waker, and to stupe more ivry year.

Yeou ax me about "Master Charley". Well, he growed up such a pretty bor. He lived along with my mother for the most part, and Mr. James was so fond of him. He'd come down, and pläa and talk to him the hour togither, and Master Charley would foller 'im about like a little dawg.

One däa they was togither, and Owd Master met 'em. "James," said he, "what bor is that alluz follerin' yeou about?" He said, "It's Mary's child." The owd man târned round as if he'd bin shot, and went home all himpin' along. Folks heared him säa, "Mary's child! Lord! Lord!" When he got in, he sot down, and nivver spôok a wâdd, 'cept now and then, "Mary's child! Lord! Lord!" He coun't ate no dinner; but he towd 'em to go for my mother; and when she come, he säa to her, "Missus, yeou must git me to bed." And there he läa all night, nivver släpin' a bit, but goin' on säain, "Mary's child! Lord! Lord!" quite solemn like. Sumtimes he'd säa, "I've bin a bad 'un in my time, I hev."

Next mornin' Mr. James sent for the doctor. But when he come, Owd Master said, "Yeou can do nothin' for me; I oon't take none o' yar stuff." No more he would. Then Mr. James säa, "Would yeou like to see the parson?" He din't säa nothin' for some time, then he said, "Yeou may send for him." When the parson come – and he was a nice quite owd gentleman, we were werry fond of him – he went up and stää'd some time; but he nivver said nôthin' when he come down. Howsomdiver, Owd Master läa more quiter arter that, and when they axed him to take his med'cin he took it. Then he slep' for some hours, and when he woke up he called out quite clear, "James." And when Mr. James come, he säa to him, "James," sez he, "I ha' left iverything to yeou; do you see that Mary hev her share." You notiz, he din't säa, "Mary's child," but "Mary hev her share." Arter a little while he said, "James, I should like to see the little chap." He warn't far off, and my mother made him tidy, and brushed his hair, and parted it. Then she took him up, and put him close to the bed. Owd Master bod 'em put the curtain back, and he läa and looked at Master Charley. And then he said, quite slow and tendersome, "Yeou're a'most as pritty as your mother was, my dear."

Them was the last words he ivver spôok.

Mr. James nivver married, and when he died he left ivrything to Master Charley.

Robert Hindes Groome quoted by Francis Hindes Groome,
Two Suffolk Friends

4. THE WAVENEY

> *Listen to me –*
> *There is a little river, fed by rills*
> *That winds among the hills,*
> *And turns and suns itself unceasingly,*
> *And wanders through the cornfields wooingly,*
> *For it has nothing else to do, but play*
> *Along its cheery way:*
> *Not like great rivers that in locks are bound,*
> *On whom hard man doth heavy burdens lay,*
> *And fret their waters into foam and spray.*
> *This river's life is one long holiday*
> > *All the year round.*
>
> *Listen and long –*
> *It hears the bells of many churches chime,*
> *It has a pleasant time:*
> *The trees that bow to it their branches strong,*
> *Hide many birds that make its spring one song;*
> *And orchard boughs let fall their flowery wealth,*
> *To float away by stealth,*
> *And land in tiny coves a mile below,*
> *Or round and round the stems of rushes veer*
> *Like snowy foam, but truly none is here,*
> *So calmly gurgle on the waters clear*
> > *With endless flow.*

Jean Ingelow

5. NEAR THE COAST

Turning to joys enhanced by the elements of roused imagination, how often have I sat musing among the spreading boughs of a great old Spanish chestnut-tree (somehow associated in my boyish mind with the Armada), whence the view of the pleasant Playford hollow included a few acres of reedy marsh known as "the mere": a name that stirred my imagination mightily, and I can well remember how I tried in vain – for this mere had no open water – to make it serve me for King Arthur's death-scene, or how anon, having had the idea thrust upon me that its mud was 'bottomless', I would convert it into a morass tragically fraught with histories of engulfed armies.

In moods like this the knowledge of the sea's neighbourhood to our home, and of its sending twice a day its marginal waters inland, flooding the mud-banks of the estuaries, and lifting and stroking back their water-weeds, until it was met by the outflow of our meadow streams, – this knowledge helped to dilate the childish spirit with a sense of ulterior mystery, and of the possibility of great world-voyages lying not remotely beyond the horizon lines. I remember this sense receiving a queer special point and significance from the fact that not far from the place where our two brooks, the Lark and the Fynn, having run together into one, broaden out to form a tidal creek of the Deben, there stood a public house having for sign a grotesque carved and scarlet-painted head and shoulders of a red lion (The Red Lion of Martlesham) which had served, we knew, in old time as the figure-head of an ocean-going ship.

Sir Sidney Colvin, *Memories and Notes of Persons and Places*

6. A STORMY REGION

All that region was full of strange rumor for a child. Not far was the famous old coaching inn, the Red Lion at Martlesham, whose vermilion-painted sign was said to be a figurehead cast ashore from the storm-driven Armada of Spain. Years afterward he saw a painting which perfectly recorded the lonely and foreboding aspect of that elbow of the stream. It was called "Storm over Martlesham Heath", and he experienced again those cumulated purple clouds and metal sky seen in late afternoon when he was far from home. The little church at Martlesham was minutely clear in such a stormy light; a blue tint of menace glittered on the obsidian leaves of an enormous holly hedge. It seemed a thorny shield to protect church and rectory from any current of wider air.

So, like the Thorofare, the River was a narrow channel leading back into something fabulously old. It runs its modest course with many windings from the primrose beds of Melton to the salt-stained shark's teeth of Bawdsey Ferry; from the lyrics of Tennyson to the barbed wire and tank traps of the pebbly coast. To be carried downstream with a fair breeze in Harry Bredfield's sailboat for a picnic at Bawdsey was a dozen miles easy sailing; if the breeze was contrary or tide miscalculated, getting back again was a long affair. The round Martello towers still stood along that shore. Faded and lichened, they were a memento of threatened invasion long ago.

There was a moment of sun and wind and high tide when Uncle Dan paused at a bend in the river wall, looked up toward the strong flint tower of Wilford Church and the last of the old windmills on the ridge, and said bashfully,

"Is this the hill, is this the kirk,

Is this mine own countree?"

He then turned back toward the Thorofare in the apologetic silence of the Englishman who has shown his emotions.

Christopher Morley, *Thorofare*

7. CHILDHOOD MEMORIES

Looking back, as I was saying, into the blank of my infancy, the first objects I can remember as standing out by themselves from a confusion of things, are my mother and Peggotty. What else do I remember? Let me see.

There comes out of the cloud, our house – not new to me, but quite familiar, in its earliest remembrance. On the ground-floor is Peggotty's kitchen, opening into a back yard; with a pigeon house on a pole, in the centre, without any pigeons in it; a great dog-kennel in a corner, without any dog; and a quantity of fowls that look terribly tall to me, walking about in a menacing and ferocious manner. There is one cock who gets upon a post to crow, and seems to take particular notice of me as I look at him through the kitchen window, who makes me shiver, he is so fierce. Of the geese outside the side-gate who come waddling after me with their long necks stretched out when I go that way, I dream at night; as a man environed by wild beasts might dream of lions.

Here is a long passage – what an enormous perspective I make of it! – leading from Peggotty's kitchen to the front-door. A dark store-room opens out of it, and that is a place to be run past at night; for I don't know what may be among those tubs and jars and old tea-chests, when there is nobody in there with a dimly-burning light, letting a mouldy air come out at the door, in which there is the smell of soap, pickles, pepper, candles and coffee, all at one whiff. Then there are the two parlours; the parlour in which we sit of an evening, my mother and I and Peggotty – for Peggotty is quite our companion, when her work is done and we are alone – and the best parlour where we sit on a Sunday; grandly, but not so comfortably. There is something of a doleful air about that room to me, for Peggotty has told me – I don't know when, but apparently ages ago – about my father's funeral, and the company having their black cloaks put on. On Sunday night my mother reads to Peggotty and me in there, how Lazarus was raised up from the dead. And I am so frightened that they are afterwards obliged to take me out of bed, and show me the quiet churchyard out of the bedroom window, with the dead all lying in their graves at rest, below the solemn moon.

There is nothing half so green that I know anywhere, as the grass of that churchyard; nothing half so shady as its trees; nothing half so quiet as its tombstones. The sheep are feeding there, when I kneel up, early in the morning, in my little bed in a closet within my mother's room, to look out at it; and I see the red light shining on the sun-dial, and think within myself, 'Is the sun-dial glad, I wonder, that it can tell the time again?'

Charles Dickens, *David Copperfield*

8. THE ORWELL

> *Of Philip de Broke, of 'Chesapeake' fame;*
> *Of Candish who sailed round the world O.*
> *Of Vernon who hatefully watered the rum.*
> *(They nicknamed the felon 'Old Grog O')*
> *But more than all these, I tell of a star*
> *Which shines in the East like a jewel.*
> *Sparkling enchantingly down to the sea*
> *The wonder of Suffolk – The Orwell.*

Anon

9. ACROSS THE ALDE

My greatest treat was a trip to Aldeburgh. For this I was allowed to borrow a governess cart, driven by an elderly groom with Dundreary whiskers and the good Suffolk name of Pryke (I suppose that the housekeeper in 'Albert Herring' was really Miss Pryke, but Miss Pike is easier to sing). We would drive to a point opposite Slaughden where a large bell hung from a wooden gibbet. If one rang it long enough a man would row over, grumbling, and take one back. I would then walk to Aldeburgh, have tea at Reading's, and spend the rest of the afternoon on the beach looking for amber, which of course I never found, and collecting pocketfuls of pebbles, which of course lost their lustre by the time I got them home. I usually ended by buying a small piece of amber in Mr. Stephenson's shop.

The charm of Aldeburgh is very difficult to define, as I often find when I try to persuade an American or Italian friend to visit the festival. I could not explain to my parents why I liked it so much, and they were slightly annoyed by my frequent requests to go there. For some reason I had got it into my head that this was a place where my wits were brighter and my senses more alert than anywhere else.

I have never lost this feeling; and when, almost forty years later, there was a reason for going there again, I felt sure that a piece of myself would be recovered. To my astonishment it had hardly changed, and I found that I, too, had changed much less than I had expected: I immediately began to look for amber, although by this time I knew quite well that I should never find it; and I brought back even larger handfuls of fast-fading stones. I found that the delicate music of the Suffolk coast, with its woods straggling into sandy commons, its lonely marshes and estuaries full of small boats, still had more charm for me than the great brass bands of natural scenery, the Alps or the Dolomites. To all this was added the fact that Benjamin Britten had settled there, and made it a centre of inspiration. Others are better qualified than I am to understand the technical mastery of Ben's music; but in so far as it takes some of its colouring from the sea, the skies and marshes of East Suffolk, I can claim to be an initiate. Grimes and Herring are my compatriots.

Kenneth Clarke, 'The Other Side of the Alde' in *A Tribute to Benjamin Britten on his 50th Birthday*

10. HARRY PAGE

The Page family must be as old as any in the district. They can point to graves dating back for many generations. My two friends in the family are brothers, now in their 'eighties but still known to my landlady as "the boys". It is the elder of the two, recently retired from regular work as a labourer at the age of eighty-one, who is good enough to come occasionally to put the garden to rights.

In spite of his age, Harry Page remains a wonderfully good worker. With the method of a life-long labourer he never appears to hurry, and yet he does a job quicker and a great deal better than ever I could do. I am indeed fortunate in having his help, since his services are much in request.

Page is a fine looking man, still straight and never without his bowler hat which on Sunday is replaced by another somewhat smarter in appearance. There is nothing incongruous in Page's wearing of a bowler hat as he walks through the Forest: this headgear was, after all, universal in his youth. Indeed, if any man has the right to wear what he likes there, it is Page. He was born in the farm in the valley within a stone's-throw and has worked near and walked in the Forest all his days.

Page started work – bird-scaring and stone picking for the most part – at the age of seven and a half, over seventy years ago; his working life is by no means finished. There were ten children in the family and he tells me that they rarely had meat except on Sundays. In those days, before the Ground Game Acts were passed, tenant farmers had no right to catch and kill rabbits which would have helped the food supply.

The farm is very small and most of the land is poor. The tenant had to work very hard to make a bare living. The children had bread and cheese, vegetables, eggs, and fruit in season. There was plenty of milk and butter, for a few cows were kept. Though they probably fed better than do most people on today's rations, they often went to bed hungry. Yet they all but two grew up to be strong men and women and to do useful jobs in the world. One cannot wish that such conditions of life should return; but that is no reason for withholding a full mead of admiration for the people that they produced.

Page graduated from bird-scarer to shepherd's boy and was presently promoted to be a sort of general help at the Hall. Here he earned half a crown a week and was fed; but he had to provide his own clothes. Eventually, failing to gain a rise in pay, he took a labourer's job elsewhere. Even in those days he found that it was difficult to dress himself on a wage of twelve pounds a year.

When Page's father died he and a brother tried to carry on the farm. But the times were against them, and after a few years they were forced to give up their tenancy. The men for the most part became labourers; one took up game-keeping. So ended a tradition of yeomanry that had lasted for I do not know how many generations. Such stories are common in the countryside.

Work on the farm was, as I have said, very hard: to yield well the sandy soil needs heavy dunging and constant hoeing. Often enough a drought meant a ruined crop. The land would grow very little wheat, but it would carry some rye and barley. The meadows required constant attention in the way of ditch-clearing and the spreading of sand to keep down the growth of rushes. This sand was dug from the pits in and near the Forest.

Sheep, in those days before refrigeration, were the mainstay of the light lands. It was the arrival of imported meat as much as the rise in wages that made farming the light lands unprofitable. Their golden hooves had meant a great deal to the economy of farming.

I think that it was in his early days of shepherding that Page gained his love of reading. He tells me that he likes nothing so much as to take his book, of a Sunday or upon a summer's evening, and to sit on a log or against one of the trees in the Thicks. The whole atmosphere of the place, including its peculiar scent, is very dear to him. There is a savour in this of Pepys' description of the shepherd and his lad reading the Bible together on the Downs. The two old men, separated in time by over two and a half centuries, would, I feel, have found much in common.

It is the old novelists he likes best and, of course, the Bible. He has little use for the novels that his daughter gets for him from the library.

Country people are apt to be inarticulate, so that they give the impression that they are unconscious of the beauties that surround them. Sometimes that may be so, but, talking to Page, one soon realises his deep love of the countryside, its sights, scents, and sounds. This love is entirely natural and artless. His face has a remarkably serene expression, a rare thing in these days because so few people with the necessary understanding are able to live close to nature in our surburban age. Never rich, his pleasures have been in simple things, such as the red rose that he planted last autumn. (He trudged a couple of miles to get a bucketful of clay to ensure that it should have the best chance.) His life has, I think, with his natural nobility of character, been a happy one.

Hugh Farmar, *The Cottage in the Forest*

11. SUFFOLK FOREST

At the end of the avenue we came to that fragment of a haunted forest which is near as old as measured history, a very part of England's time and bone. It is so old that the New Forest is no more than an upstart beside this wood of twisted trees and climbing mistletoe. It was here when the Druids raised their skinny arms to the sun, and blood ran on the altars of Stonehenge.

A keeper's cottage crouches at its edge, thatched and diamond-paned, in a little garden full of hollyhocks and brown and red autumn flowers. The forest comes up to it with wrinkled, reaching arms. You must be a man of no imagination to sleep well in that cottage.

In the forest there is silence. The feet sink into leaf-mould so deep that a stick goes in to the crook. The trees over-arch and soar. They are huge and gnarled – grotesque and eerily beautiful. A haunted place of strangely living trees, so old that man to them is a joke, a plaything of time. Oak and birch, beech and ivy, hoary mistletoe and gigantic holly – all are supernormal trees, beyond any I have seen in girth and age and sheer fantasy. It is a Hans Andersen wood, a place grimmer than Grimm, a place which you may picture as any fantastic theatre stage you please – a devil's abode, a monkish pleasance, a place of ghosts and woodland witch-craft, a hidden, lost echo of that old England of Giloas the Celt and Asserius the Saxon, which still hides here and there in forgotten pockets of the countryside. It is a place of the old gods, a place sacred before Christ walked on Galilee, a place so old that its memories are forgotten, its old gods blown whispers down the aisles of an older Britain that died when the Roman came . . .

The keeper's cottage was drawing into the shadow of its thatch-bonnet for the night. Pheasants crowed and cock-upped to roost. Dogs jingled their chains in the kennels at the back. And, far back in the forest, the fantastic football-ground of the gods was alone with its dim echo of ghostly laughter, the clink of Parnassian armour.

Memory went back to another evening in that old forest of the tree-faces. A winter day's pigeon-shooting with Suffolk farmers. Pigeons bronze and oddly pink against the high glow of a red evening sun. Pigeons circling in, high as angels, or sitting, wary as monkeys, on the tops of tall, bare trees. Frosty hedges and rimy roads with a white snow-mist on the stubbles and a great cock-pheasant, red-eyed and brilliant, strutting like a rajah.

I thought of that evening's pigeon-flight as we walked back under the great beech avenue, its pale, towering trunks soaring into the leafy vaults above the tanks.

"Some one who comes after me must replant this avenue", he said.

"These beeches are too good to lose, and they won't last more than another forty or fifty years.'

The Priory, his re-creation, rose out of the ground mist, greyly silver, like a great earthbound moth resting lightly on the grass where the King's deer had trod.

Long after the tanks have rusted and the bombers are a nightmare the thoughts and deeds of that scholarly lover of ancient beauty will endure.

James Wentworth Day, *Harvest Adventure*

12. The Blythe

Yesterday I half believed that the winter drew to its end; the breath of the hills was soft; spaces of limpid pure azure shone amid the slow-drifting clouds, and seemed the promise of spring. Idle by the fireside, in the gathering dusk, I began to long for the days of light and warmth. My fancy wandered, leading me far and wide in a dream of summer England . . .

This is the valley of the Blythe. The stream ripples and glances over its brown bed warmed with sunbeams; by its bank the green flags wave and rustle, and, all about, the meadows shine in pure gold of buttercups. The hawthorn hedges are a mass of gleaming blossom, which scents the breeze. There above rises the heath, yellow-mantled with gorse, and beyond, if I walk for an hour or two, I shall come out upon the sandy cliffs of Suffolk and look over the northern sea . . .

George Gissing, *The Private Papers of Henry Ryecroft*

13. From the Coast

For Stour, a daintie flood, that duly doth divide
Fair Suffolke from this shire, upon her other side;
By Clare first comming in, to Sudbury doth show,
The even course she keepes; when farre she doth not flow,
But Breton a bright nymph, fresh succour to her brings:
Yet is she not so proud of her superfluous springs,
But Orwell comming in from Ipswitch thinkes that shee,
Should stand for it with Stour, and lastly they agree,
That since the Britans hence their first discoveries made,
And that into the east they first were taught to trade.
Besides, of all the roads, and havens of the east,
This harbor where they meet, is reckoned for the best.

Michael Drayton, *Poly-Olbion*

14. TRAVELLING

All the other roads were parish ones, maintained by the separate villages
as far as their boundary, until we were grouped in Highway Boards.
Material for mending them was gathered from the fields, because our clay
soil was well sprinkled with small flints, and though flints are not the best
stuff for roads they would have done fairly well had they been rolled. But
steam rollers were unknown, and since all vehicles were made of the same
width so as to 'run in the track', for half the year we expected to find three
lines in the road made by the near wheel, the horses and the off wheel. If
the road were wide enough and much used there would be five lines. It
was hard on the horses who had to drag loads over the new-laid metal,
and they often fell lame by picking up a stone in the foot.

The life on our roads was among the great interests of the country. A
fast trotter was the delight of everyone who saw it go by. To quote
Borrow . . . "A Norfolk cob to ride" was the ideal mount. They were
splendid animals, and John Grout, of the Bull Inn at Woodbridge, had a
strain of hackneys which would bear comparison with the best in
England. In the good times farmers liked to have something that was hard
to pass when they drove to market, and those who could not afford one of
the highest class in shape and action would seek something fast, even if it
were but a 'powny', and pay a good sum for it too, though they did
bargain long over the deal. One very pretty little dun mare with black
points was purchased after long negotiations for 'a cow and a calf, five
pounds and some hay'; rather a difficult sum to work out, but the pur-
chaser boasted of his bargain.

The distances travelled in the course of a week by many people, and
the hours they spend in their carts, were almost more than we can
imagine. Dealers, especially those in the pig trade, and the higglers who
bought eggs and chickens, the sweeps, whose circuit was very wide (for
that was an occupation in which there was very little competition), the
exciseman, the country doctors, the butchers and the drivers of the
grocers' carts, all must have horses which could go far every day for six
days in the week.

James Cornish, *Reminiscences of Country Life*

15. THE CRINKLE CRANKLE WALL

Gardens and orchards. There is nothing in this branch of culture, that has
come to my knowledge, that seems to claim particular attention; without
doubt, there are practices in the county which would be worthy of inser-
tion, had they been communicated. I have only to observe one practice,

not common elsewhere, which is, that of building garden walls no more than the breadth of a common brick in thickness, by means of waving the line. The saving is considerable. In regard to the effect, both in point of duration and fruit, accounts are various; and the introduction of this method is not of a sufficient date, to ascertain it satisfactorily.

Arthur Young, *General View of the Agriculture of the County of Suffolk*

16. THE VILLAGE SMOKER

It chanced sometimes, that when out for an evening run with some of my fellow members of the Ipswich Bicycle Club, we would come across a number of rustics, supported probably by a few farmers' sons, holding a 'sing-song' in the parlour of a village inn. There was often a good deal of amusement to be extracted from an occasion of this kind. Sometimes the Parson's and the Squire's sons took a hand in the revels, or at any rate gave encouragement to the performers. Most of their songs had an old English flavour, and some would hardly pass muster in a society drawing-room. Yet most were quite harmless and entirely moral.

I can remember scraps of two of them, which were popular items on such occasions, and certainly amusing. One was about a farmer which commenced as follows:—

"There was an old farmer in Suffolk did dwell.
Tally I ho! yer know!
He had an old wife and he wished her (not well),
Tally I ho! Yer know!

One day old Nick met him at the Plough,
Tally I ho! yer know!
Said he 'One of your crowd must come with me now!'
Tally I ho! yer know!

Oh, do not take my eldest son,
Tally I ho! yer know!
If you do, kind devil, I'm hully undone,
Tally I ho! yer know!

It's not yer eldest son I crave,
Tally I ho! yer know!
But yer snarling beast of a wife I will have,
Tally I ho! yer know!

With that he bundled her into a sack,
Tally I ho! yer know!

And like a proud pedlar he shouldered his pack
Tally I ho! yer know!

So the verses were strung out to cover the whole story, and there was, of course, a rollicking chorus after each verse. For the curious I might add that the black imp was supposed to take the lady off to the regions below. Here she made herself so objectionable that his satanic majesty was only too glad to return her, carriage paid, to the disappointed family circle.

For another song a red-headed, brown-faced son of the soil had donned the proverbial smock, and gave his admiring audience an account of his amorous adventures. The chorus of this ran as follows:—

> *"Mary Anne she's arter me!*
> *Full o'-luv she seems to be.*
> *My mither says it's 'plain tew see*
> *She wants yer for her young man*
> *Feather says 'If that be trew,*
> *John, my boy, be thankful dew,*
> *There's one bigger fool in the world than yew,*
> *That's Ma-a-a-rey Anne!"*

O. R. Wellbanks, *Suffolk, My County*

17. A Move to Suffolk

My wife's health having caused me to petition to be removed to Suffolk, my wish was kindly granted, and I have never regretted that migration. Northerners are warm-hearted and hospitable, but the spirit they vaunt so loudly as independence manifests itself not unfrequently in a rawness of manner that amounts to insolence. The wheels of life are better oiled in the pleasanter surroundings of Suffolk where the native is of a naturally courteous turn of mind.

The moorland strip stretching between Felixstowe and Sandringham, some ten miles inland, is canopied by a bluer sky and carpeted by a drier soil during a longer period of the year than any other part of England. Although this soil is geologically akin to that of Bournemouth, the air makes that of the favourite health resort seem faint and languid in comparison. Visitors who have seen Suffolk from the window of a railway carriage can have but an inadequate idea of the charm of that moorland strip, parts of which the Ordnance Map so well dubs "Little Scotland", "New Delight" etc, and at both ends of which royalty has chosen a residence – Edward III at Felixstowe, Edward VII at Sandringham. Full many a Tintern-like structure, full many a glorious old church furnish additional proof of the appreciation of bygone generations.

A. Swinburn, *Memories of a School Inspector*

18. VILLAGE CONCERTS

Mummie must have suffered much from her gift of music, for to her fell the task of training a crude country choir – the Suffolk people are not musical – and of playing the accompaniments for village songsters when our next-door neighbour, dear Admiral Aldrich, organised monthly concerts which were held in the village Recreation Room during the winter. How well I remember those rehearsals held in our Rectory schoolroom; and those rumpty-tumpty accompaniments to the comic songs which had to be repeated, sometimes twenty times, until the singer removed his collar the better to reach a high note. Mummie got the maddening tunes so badly on the brain that she was unable to sleep, and would go downstairs to her piano in the small hours to play them out of her head. But the villagers loved those concerts so much that it was worth the agony; the walls streamed with condensed heat, and the light from the swinging oil-lamps shone down upon the beaming rubicund faces of familiar friends who stamped their applause until one wondered if the floorboards could withstand so much enthusiasm.

From very early days 'Miss Winnie' was expected to recite to this appreciative audience, who thought her amateur efforts marvels of talent.

Daddie gave humorous readings, Marjory danced hornpipes and Irish jigs learned at her dancing class; the Admiral sang ballads in a sweet tenor voice; really good orchestral music and solos were played by the Downing family, Mrs. Downing at the piano, Maud with a violin, Dolly with her viola and Jessie with her cello.

Most of the audience did not understand good music, and the village lads at the back of the room were apt to converse with the village lasses during these numbers, and, at the conclusion of a very lovely violin solo played by Maud Downing, her mother closed the piano with a bang and remarked with an acid smile: "Maud tried to play as softly as possible so as not to interrupt the talking."

Winifred Fortescue, *There's Rosemary . . . There's Rue*

19. STRAW-PLAITING

Another village activity with which Mark and Jessie were both familiar from their earliest years was straw-plaiting. In later years, Jessie was to become (as Mark expressed it) "the championest braider in the village"; and he himself has never lost his skill in the allied arts of plaiting dollies, frames and bonds. In the actual industry of straw-plaiting, as practised by his mother when he was a boy, and by most other mothers in the village, he never seems to have taken much part. I suspect that such a docile task was uncongenial to his quick blood and agile limbs. Yet in most families, at that time, not only the mother but also her children would (at least intermittently) be occupied in plaiting straw into "scores" of "wisp", "whip-cord" or "brilliant". Any of the older inhabitants of Larkfield will tell how the women sat at their open doors in summer, or walked slowly up and down the roadway, weaving the straws together without even bothering to look at them, and busily talking to one another as they worked; whilst in winter it did not matter that the glimmering rush-light candle was all their light, because their expert fingers could almost have plaited in the dark. The braid would be wound round a half-yard measure, taken off so that it sprang back into coils of a yard each, tied together and labelled with a piece of paper saying how much and of what kind. These coils the women carried over their shoulders to the village, where, on an appointed day each week, a collector called, counted the number of coils each woman handed in (and hence the number of yards), and departed with his profitable load. At the height of the boom in straw-plaiting, I have heard it said, this collector might take out of the village as much as a hundred pounds' worth of braid. The price paid to the cottager was usually about sevenpence or eightpence a "score" – though Mark declared it occasionally rose to as much as tenpence. Deftly fingered women, aided by their children, could plait a good "score" a day, and so were able to earn almost as much money at home as their men-folk out in the fields.

Mark and his wife explained the whole process to me one day as I sat in his cottage, the morning sunlight blazing on a scarlet cactus in his window and a thrush singing loudly from one of the elm-trees outside. "It's like this," Mark began. "First of all you had to pick out your straw, and only the best and finest would do. Of course it had to be scythed or sickled straw – the binder don't cut it off long enough. Most of the straw was bought from the local farmers, though as I've told you afore quite a number of the cottagers had a few rod of wheat of their own. Them that had their own wheat used to chop off the heads for frailin', put the straw in sacks, and store it away in the cottage somewhere till it was wanted, or in a shed or a lean-to, anywhere that was safe from vermin, if they *had* such a place! Then, when the time came, the straw was cut into lengths – 'strippings' we called 'em – and bleached. Can you guess how that was done? Well, you got hold of a barrel, or anythin' suitable, and stood the strippings round in a circle. Then you put a lump of sulphur or brimstone on a tin lid, lighted it, lowered it down into the middle of the barrel, and covered it all over with a bit of sacking.

"You wouldn't think you could split a straw into ten parts, would you?" Mark continued. "Of course, that was only for very fine work. You split it on an 'engine' – a little contrivance that could be set to the number of split straws you happened to want. You pressed the straw down over

the point of this engine and the blades did all the rest for you. Then you
held the straws in a bunch between your second and third fingers, like so;
drew 'em through your teeth, so's they got wetted with the spit; and then
went ahead with the braidin'. But – " Mark paused, as if the concentration
on so much detail had suddenly bored him. He rose from his chair.
"What am I thinkin' of?" he said. "Won't you take a glass of wine?"

While he was away, choosing a bottle from under the table in the next
room, Mrs. Thurston fetched a drying-cloth from the scullery and began
wiping a couple of tumblers, holding them up to the light as she did so, to
make sure no speck of dust remained on them. "Yes," she said in her
rather prim, small voice, "I've made hats for the Queen. At least, I've
helped to make the straw-plait for them. The most difficult plaiting of all
was called 'brilliant'; and for that you had to split your straws into fourteen strands, so you can imagine how tricky it was to handle. They had a
school for plaiting once, in the village. The girls paid in twopence or
threepence a week. But the whole business of straw-plaiting fell to pieces
while I was still a young woman; I don't know for why. Prices got so low
as fourpence a score; and that wasn't worth anybody's while, was it?"

C. Henry Warren, Happy Countryman

20. Eating, Drinking and 'Parge'

Now commenced the absorbing, exciting yet serious game of finding a
suitable farm.

It must have a good, roomy house to accommodate the large family
which every young couple expected as a matter of course. It must have
land in good heart; not too light, as is some of the soil near the Suffolk
coast. Good pasture as well as arable, and ample buildings, as Henry had
confided to Emely his ambition to establish a stud of Suffolk Punches,
which should bring him fame and fortune, and a herd of Red Polls, from
which he could one day cull a prize-winner.

The farm must not be too far from the Essex and Suffolk country, and
near enough to get a sniff, from the sea and salt mud, of the ozone which
was the breath of life to them both.

As luck would have it, the very thing near at hand, at Kirton, was
becoming vacant at Michaelmas. Michaelmas in those days was the 11th
of October.

Although it did not afford all they wanted, no one must expect just
everything in this wonderful world.

Emely would have preferred the working part of the house more con-
veniently arranged. The châtelaine of a large farm had to supervise the
work of what was really a manufactory in miniature.

The beer was brewed at home – large quantities were required for the
house and the farm hands. All sorts of home-made wines were prepared

and bottled – parsnip, mangold, elderberry, dandelion, cowslip and parsley. Little or no cider was made, as cider apples do not thrive in Suffolk, and this wine industry took the place corresponding to that of cider in other counties.

Amongst the few things I have of my grandfather's is a copper vessel for making punch. Conical in shape, it holds nearly a quart. The wine or beer, spiced and sugared to taste, was put into this muller and the pointed end was stuck into the wood embers and the contents heated to the required temperature.

A hundred years ago mulled wine was largely drunk, and was served in the best inns. Mulled port was called 'Bishop'; if you preferred mulled claret, you demanded the 'Cardinal'. Should burgundy be your choice, you would order nothing less than the 'Pope'. The Church then knew what was good for the body as well as the soul. At what date, and why, did it discard the advice of Saint Paul to Timothy?

Quantities of butter had to be made weekly, the surplus being salted down for winter use. Hams and bacon were cured and smoked up the chimneys, in special bacon cupboards. Suffolk sugar-cured hams and bacon were famous well into the last century, and only during the past few decades has this delicacy become almost forgotten.

The bread was baked on the premises in the large bake-oven, a feature of the 'backhus' (back kitchen) of every farmhouse. The large iron oven door opened into the kitchen fireplace. The method of baking was first to put faggots into the oven itself, and set them on fire. The oven door was then left open; there was no flue, and the smoke went up the chimney of the ordinary fireplace. The hot embers were left in as long as they generated heat, then raked out, the bottom of the oven being wiped with a damp rag tied to a stick.

The oven was then at a considerable temperature, and the bread, cakes, meat pies, fruit tarts, and other dainties, sufficient for a week's supply, were put in.

The bread, in shape what we now know as 'cottage loaf', was placed in the oven with long-handled flat shovels called 'peels'. The dough was kneaded the day before in an oak or elm receptacle, called a dough trough (something like a cradle on legs), part of the furniture of every kitchen. The bottom of the oven on which the bread was placed was made of hard brick, but the walls were lined with parge, which we should now think an extraordinarily constituted material for the interior of a cooking range. I may put some people off eating anything cooked in an old bake-oven when I give the recipe for parge:

Take one part sand, half part lime, add sufficient water and mix into a paste. Then take one part cow-dung, as fresh as possible and mix well all ingredients. This makes a plaster which does not crack, is retentive of heat, and will last for years.

Even now, in the country, the old bricklayers use this preparation for lining flues.

George Cross, *Suffolk Punch*

21. STRAIGHT THROUGH

The meadows lying along the banks of the Waveny (which passes through them with an even, gentle course) are supposed to be among the richest in England. Here besides the cattle of the country, numerous herds of starved cattle from the highlands of Scotland, find their way. Of such pasturage they had no idea. Here they lick up grass by mouthfulls: the only contention is, which of them can eat the most, and grow fat the soonest. When they have gotten smooth coats, and swagging sides, they continue their journey to the capital, and present themselves in Smithfield, where they find many admirers.

About eight miles before we reach Ipswich, the country assumes a more variegated face. The village of Stoneham, which stands high, incompassed with wood, makes a picturesque appearance from the opposite hill.

The country still improves as we approach Ipswich, but chiefly in near views. Pleasing woody scenes open first on one hand; and then on the other; villas and villages adorn the landscape on every side; and here and there, a beautiful distance opens, which was now become a novelty.

About the seventh stone Mr. Bacon's at Codenham, affords a scene of noble oaks rising on the left, a little above the road. His house just opens, and shuts, among the trees, as we glide past.

Ipswich is a large, incumbered, unpleasant place. The market-house is an old rotunda, supported by wooden pillars, with a figure of justice on the top. The form is not unpleasing.

On leaving Ipswich we took the Colchester road, through sandy, heavy lanes. The country is like what we had left; but in a less picturesque style of landscape. About six miles from Ipswich the lanes open upon a woody scene, which looks like the skirts of some vast forest.

This scenery being removed, the road is adorned with two or three beautiful dips, on the left, interspersed with cottages, and a variety of fine wood. Beyond these is a good distance. Soon after the tower of Dedham-church makes a picturesque appearance.

Having presented us with all these views, the road suddenly shuts in all objects; dives into a shady bottom; and carries us into Stratford St. Mary's; which is the last town in Suffolk.

The cattle, through all this country, are a beautiful breed of cream-coloured beasts, without horns.

William Gilpin, *Observations on Several Parts of the Counties of Norfolk, Suffolk and Essex*

22. MUCK CARTING

Forty years ago, too, when a farmer came to buy a new farm, one of the things that he looked for on his first visit of inspection was the depth of the muck in the yards. If it was less than a foot deep, he generally thought again before he bought the farm. At Peyton Hall, in old Mr. Waller's day, the muck was a good eighteen inces to two feet deep before it was carted. Yet the top layer was always sweet and clean straw for, every week throughout the year, except in the hottest days in summer, fresh straw was pitched into the yards, loads and loads of it, and roughly spread around so that there was no part where the old straw was still actually uncovered. The horses themselves were the best agents for spreading the straw for, when they were turned out of their stable after 'bait' in the evening, it was no uncommon sight to see all the twenty or two dozen of them rolling on their backs, flattening the straw out. In this way they rubbed freshness into their skins; but, as the week went on, and the straw became fouled by their defecations and urinations, you would notice that the horses did not roll so frequently as when the straw was first fresh. And all the time they were stamping their ordure and urine into the straw where it sank through to the bottom, rotting it all thoroughly, so that when the time of the muck-carting came, all the lower part of the once golden straw had assumed the rich colour and consistency of an old-fashioned plum pudding.

Generally, there would be about half a dozen single horse tumbrils in use at a time at a muck-carting. That meant six horses were being used and eight to a dozen men, for two men at least were needed to pitch the muck into the tumbrils while only one man was wanted for the unloading on the actual field. This unloading was always started by a very long and unwieldy two-pronged fork which the men used to pull the muck into little heaps, at intervals of about ten yards, on the ground. A good tumbril-load produced about four little heaps. At the last heap, however, the fork was not used, but a pin, which held the body of the tumbril in a level position while it was in place, was pulled out, the horse was told to 'git up' and then 'whoa!' and the body of the tumbril turned vertically sideways and the remaining muck fell on to the last of the four piles.

It was at muck-carting and the carting at harvest home that even a small boy such as myself could be of real use, for very often each load had to be carried as much as half a mile or a mile from the yard to its destination: and a load of well-rotted sodden manure might weigh almost a ton, so that the speed at which it could be hauled even over fields that had had all the summer sun on them was never more – and often less – than four miles an hour. Consequently, if there was a body handy who could take the load from the yard to the field, he released a man who could either stay in the yard loading or on the field unloading.

This was where I came into my kingdom.

Simon Dewes, *A Suffolk Childhood*

23. MEMORIES

Reuben is always glad of an opportunity to talk and even recite, has a ready flow of wit and a merry laugh. His memories are of more pleasant things than bad; and his life, in retrospect, though hard, has been good to live. As I have said, he is out of the past, of the time of hand labour in the fields, of domestic economy finely practised in the home, and of hard times and heavy labour.

"Harvest time we hed tew start at five o'clock the morning', wi' a scythe in the hand all day; an' when thet wur finished up came six-pun-ten, then thet gort tew seven-pun an' seven-pun-ten. Rum owd days they wur."

"Yis, I wur born in Westleton, in thet little owd place just down the street (Mill Street). Leastways, I wur thare when I wur a little owd fella, so I spose thet's wur I wur born. When mother went a glanin' she used tew tak us in a wheelbarrer, an' my sister hed tew mind us an' see as we didn't fall out. Once the wimmin comed afore they hed clared the fild, sew they had tew wait. One owd gal say, "I can't stand sitten about hare like this!"

"My grandmother lived at Yoxford, an' one day my mother wornt well, and I had tew gew over tew grandmother and tell how she wur. I wornt wery owd thin. When I gort there she say tew me, "How's yare mother neow?""

"Thank you, grandmother" I say, "she's worse!"

... "I wur a funny little owd fella; I used tew hard folks say, 'Put yare money in the bank!' Well, thare wur a' owd bit o' bank thet runned at the back o' them cottages; sew one day I went thare, scrabbed out a hole and put my one or tew coppers in't. Later on I couldna find where I hed put it, an' fur all I know thet's thare now."

"Yes, I went tew scule until I wur about eleven. Thet wur a rare good scule then. We hed tew sing a hymn or the Doxology afore we comed out. I saw them a gittin' ridy one arternoon, sew I started up a singing afore the others, sew the master say tew me, 'Yew'll stay in till last!' One boy said suffen out o' place an' the master set intew him; an he went round the room with his leg inside a chair, sew he didna git all the cuts wi the stick.'

"The sculemaster then wur an owd fella we called owd Roger; he wore a billy-cock hat and a tail-coat, white wiskit an' a straw hat come summer, an' he believed in the stick; not many on us 'scaped that. He'd walk up the village an' beat up the stragglers, git tew scule just afore nine, gew tew his desk, pick up his cane an' pull out his watch an' wait until that wur on the stroke; then he'd swack his stick ontew the desk, pick up the tuning fork an' start us orf wi' 'Awake my soul, and with the sun', beatin' time with his stick. One o' the boys was a handful; cane evry day, until owd

Roger got tired on't, an' expelled him, sew he had tew walk tew Dunwich every day tew finish his sculeing. He wur one o' the Fisks."

"We cud make all sorts of things wi' our shut-knives. Bows an' arrows out o' the elders, an' pipes out o' straw that ud whooly make a noise. We used tew sing –

> *'Rake ye! rake ye!*
> *If ye doant squake*
> *I'll brake ye!'*

And they did squake tew."

Allan Jobson, *This Suffolk*

24. EARLIER MEMORIES

As a I lean back for another glance, my eyes, as Wordsworth writes, are filled with childish tears – 'My heart is idly stirred' – I see the dear old village where I was born, almost encroaching on Sir Thomas Gooch's park, at Benacre Hall; I see the old baronet, a fine old bigoted Tory, who looked the picture of health and happiness, as he ambled past on his chestnut cob, wearing a blue coat, a white hat and trousers, in summer; his only regret being that things were not as they were – his only consolation the fact that, wisely, the Eternal Providence that overrules all human affairs had provided snug rectories for his kith and kin, however unworthy of the sacred calling; and had hung up the sun, moon and stars so high in the heavens that no reforming ass 'Could e'er presume to pluck them down, and light the world with gas.'

Then comes the village medico, healthy and shrewd and kindly, with a firm belief – alas! that day is gone now – in black draught and blue pill. I see his six sunny daughters racing down the village street, guarded by a dragon of a governess, and I get out of their way, for I am a rustic, and have all the rustic's fear of what the East Anglian peasant was used to term "morthers"; and then comes the squire of the next parish, in as shabby a trap as you ever set eyes on, and the fat farmer, who hails me for a walk, and going to the end of a field, joyously, or as joyously as his sluggish nature will permit, exclaims, "There, Master James, now you can see three farms." My friend was a utilitarian, and could only see the beautiful in the useful. Then I call up the memory of the village grocer, a stern, unbending Radical, who delights me with the loan of Cruikshank's illustrations to the "House that Jack Built", mysteriously wrapped in brown paper and stowed away between the sugar and treacle. He does not talk much, but he thinks the more. And now it strikes me that conversation was not much cultivated in the villages of East Anglia in 1837, and yet there were splendid exceptions – on such evenings as when the members of the Book Club met in our parlour, where the best tea things were laid, and where a kindly mother in black silk and white shawl and quakerish cap made tea; where an honoured father, who now sleeps far away from the scene of his life-long labours, indulged in a genial humour, which set at ease the shyest of his guests; and again, what a splendid talk there was when the brethren in black from Beccles, from Yarmouth, from Halesworth, gathered for fraternal purposes, perhaps once a quarter, to smoke long pipes, to discuss metaphysics and politics, and to puzzle their heads over divines and systems that have long ceased to perplex the world. Few and simple were East Anglian annals then. It was seldom the London coach, the Yarmouth Mail and Telegraph brought a cockney down to astonish us with his pert ways and peculiar talk. Life was slow, but it was kindly, nevertheless.

James Ewing Ritchie, *Christopher Crayon's Recollections*

25. After the Harvest

Outside, the moon is up – the harvest moon over harvest fields. It casts a sheen upon the empty stubbles, the bare rounding slopes, so altered from the close-crowded landscape of standing corn. It has glimmering secrets among the trees, and pierces into every entanglement of foliage, and lays faint shadows across the paths. Each finds a ghost of himself beside him on the ground. An elusive radiance haunts the country; the distances have a sense of shining mist. The men move homeward from the field; the last load creaking up the hill behind them, the hoofs of the horses thudding, their breath sounding short. Peace comes, a vision in the fairy armour of moonlight, the peace of "man goeth forth unto his work until the evening."

The last load is drawn into the barn to be unloaded in the morning. The horses stand with foam on their bridles, their flanks heaving after the long pull; struggle is in their attitude. It is quite dark in the barn. There is a rattle of chains as the horses are unhitched and led away, the voices of men helping the load into position, a clatter of wood as a block is kicked under a wheel, the music of steel on steel as forks are laid together.

The men straggle out into the moonlight and pause in a group on the roadway, gazing at the sky, at the moon in her glory. (When the men pause in their work they always look at the sky.)

"Don't look much like wet," says one. "Don't want neither till that barley's out of the way."

"Looks like the colour of money to me," says another. Bob comes down from the stable. "Ho, she's regular showing off tonight," is his tribute. "Well, I'm goin' to see about some supper,' he says. There is a murmur of considered assent, as though there were something original in the idea. With gruff "Good nights" the group disperses, some going up the road, some down, and some across the fields.

The last footfall dies into silence. The stillness tingles with the aftermath of noise. All around stand the new cornstacks, unfamiliar shadows, ramparts thrown up suddenly round the yard. An owl detaches itself silently from the darkness of a beam, swoops down into the moonlight and away, now white against a shadow, now black against the moon. A mouse scuttles somewhere in the straw. The gaunt shape of a binder stands in a corner, angular as a skeleton under its cloth. Its work is over until next year.

Adrian Bell, *Corduroy*

26. A SUFFOLK PROPERTY

Suffolk is not especially a picturesque county, nor can it be said that the scenery round Carbury was either grand or beautiful; but there were little prettinesses attached to the house itself and the grounds around it which gave it a charm of its own. The Carbury River, – so called, though at no place is it so wide but that an active schoolboy might jump across it – runs, or rather creeps into the Waveney, and in its course is robbed by a moat which surrounds Carbury Manor House. The moat has been rather a trouble to its proprietors, and especially so to Roger, as in these days of sanitary considerations it has been felt necessary either to keep it clean with at any rate moving water in it, or else to fill it up and abolish it altogether. That plan of abolishing it had to be thought of and was seriously discussed about ten years since; but then it was decided that such a proceeding would altogether alter the character of the house, would destroy the gardens, and create a waste of mud all round the place which it would take years to beautify, or even to make endurable. And then an important question had been asked by an intelligent farmer who had long been a tenant on the property; 'Fill un oop; – eh, eh; sooner said than doone, squoire. Where be the stoof to come from?' The squire, therefore, had given up that idea, and instead of abolishing his moat had made it prettier than ever. The high road from Bungay to Beccles ran close to the house, – so close that the gable ends of the building were separated from it only by the breadth of the moat. A short, private road, not above a hundred yards in length, led to the bridge which faced the front door. The bridge was old, and high, with sundry architectural pretensions, and guarded by iron gates in the centre, which, however, were very rarely closed. Between the bridge and the front door there was a sweep of ground just sufficient for the turning of a carriage, and on either side of this the house was brought close to the water, so that the entrance was in a recess, or irregular quadrangle, of which the bridge and moat formed one side. At the back of the house there were large gardens screened from the road by a wall ten feet high, in which there were yew trees and cypresses said to be of wonderful antiquity. The gardens were partly inside the moat, but chiefly beyond them, and were joined by two bridges – a foot bridge and one with a carriage way, – and there was another bridge at the end of the house furthest from the road, leading from the back door to the stables and farmyard . . .

The houses of the gentry around him were superior to his in material comfort and general accommodation, but to none of them belonged that thoroughly established look of old county position which belonged to Carbury. Bundlesham, where the Primeros lived, was the finest house in that part of the county, but it looked as if it had been built within the last twenty years. It was surrounded by new shrubs and new lawns, by new walls and new outhouses, and savoured of trade; – so at least thought Roger Carbury, though he never said the words. Caversham was a very large mansion, built in the early part of George III's reign, when men did care that things about them should be comfortable, but did not care that they should be picturesque. There was nothing at all to recommend Caversham but its size. Eardly Park, the seat of the Hepworths, had, as a park, some pretensions. Carbury possessed nothing that could be called a park, the enclosures beyond the gardens being merely so many home paddocks. But the house of Eardly was ugly and bad. The Bishop's palace was an excellent gentleman's residence, but then that too was comparatively modern, and had no peculiar features of its own. Now Carbury Manor House was peculiar, and in the eyes of its owner was pre-eminently beautiful.

Anthony Trollope, The Way We Live Now

27. ANOTHER, SIMILAR

The house-warming at Low Threshold Hall was not an event that affected many people. The local newspaper, however, had half a column about it, and one or two daily papers supplemented the usual August dearth of topics with pictures of the house. They were all taken from the same angle, and showed a long, low building in the Queen Anne style flowing away from a square tower on the left which was castellated and obviously of much earlier date, the whole structure giving somewhat the impression to a casual glance of a domesticated church, or even of a small railway train that had stopped dead on finding itself in a park. Beneath the photograph was written something like 'Suffolk Manor House re-occupied after a hundred and fifty years,' . . .

To judge from the photograph, time had dealt gently with Low

Threshold Hall. Only a trained observer could have told how much of the original fabric had been renewed. The tower looked particularly convincing. While as for the gardens sloping down to the stream which bounded the foreground of the picture – they had that old-world air which gardens so quickly acquire. To see those lush lawns and borders as a meadow, that mellow brickwork under scaffolding, needed a strong effort of the imagination.

L. P. Hartley, 'Feet Foremost', from *Collected Short Stories*

28. ON THE MOVE – I

But life in Wattisham was good those spring months. Each morning the engineer section went down to a farmhouse on the other side of the field and then went out on its various jobs. The nineteen charts flourished anew, more complicated than ever, but this time with encouraging results. Before long the paver was moving steadily across the fields and through the hedgerows, and in the woods the sound of dynamite was heard where we were uprooting age-old trees, and the stockpile mountains grew with rapidity. We were old hands now at aerodrome building, for this was our second one. The big paving machine marched forward without delay.

I liked Wattisham for several reasons. This was even more beautiful countryside than that about Debach, and it was closer to Sudbury and the girl Joan. True, I had to work out new lines of communication; but I discovered that if I walked cross-country two miles to Bildeston I could catch a bus Saturday evenings that wandered through the lovely valleys to Brent Eleigh, to Lavenham, to Long Melford, and finally to Sudbury. Or I could try to hitchhike to Sudbury by the road that went down through Chelsworth and Waldingfield. Or I could go from Chelsworth across to Hadleigh and pick up my old Ipswich-Sudbury bus there. This was perhaps the most enjoyable method, and I came to know every twist and turn and every landmark along this sheltered, picturesque road.

Here there was a long hill that give a view across ten miles of rolling countryside where you could count eight church steeples. There was a stump where a little owl liked to perch in the late evening hours. Around that bend was a bean field in full bloom, its heavy, sweet fragrance pervading the air from thousands of waxy white blossoms. And at Chelsworth, one of the loveliest small villages in England, there was a small child standing at the gate who would smile and wave as I passed. It was a long hard ride, and three hills that I must walk up, but in the end I managed to cover the distance in just over an hour, and came down that last long hill into Sudbury in a whirl of speed. Swifts were screeching in the air, people were standing in their yards or clustered around 'The Pheasant' at Chelsworth or 'The Swan' at Little Waldingfield, and cars were few and far between. Three airfields were being built on that four-teen-mile stretch of road between Wattisham and Sudbury.

Coming back was more difficult. By bicycle it was uphill most of the way, and a long and lonely plod late at night, with only the hoot of tawny owls or the scream of lapwings in the fields for company. But the only other way home was to catch the evening train to Marks Tey, change for the Ipswich train, and then board the last liberty truck back to the camp. Roundabout – four hours for the fourteen miles – but then most of my travels to and from Sudbury were involved and complicated, and dependent on several modes of transport. Somehow, miraculously, I always made it back on time.

Robert Arbib, *Here We Are Together*

29. ON THE MOVE – II

(*Recollections of the "Shannon", the coach driven by old John Cole, a possible model for Dickens' Tony Weller.*)

Splendidly horsed and equipped throughout, this dear old red coach was a sight worth looking at. Old John Cole was always good to us boys when we travelled to or from school, and he endeared himself to me more especially on one occasion when travelling when cold and shivering during a bitterly cold and snowy day. He poured some 'dognose' down my throat and put me into the 'boot' under his seat, where I slept on the mail bags, warm and comfortable, for the rest of the journey.

I never pass Saxmundham Bell except with grateful recollections of that bitter journey. At the Three Tuns, Yoxford, the "Shannon" was almost invariably met by a strangely dressed woman, known to us only as 'Ninnie Fee', who seemed to be ever expecting a message or letter from a well-known nobleman of the county, and who used to tackle old John directly he descended from his box, and always waved her highly variegated parasol when the coach drove off. At the junction of the road from Aldeburgh, with the turnpike road on which we travelled, a red-painted bus, owned, I believe, by John Cole, used to meet the "Shannon" both on the up and down journey, transferring mails and passengers to and from the parent coach.

My last journey on the "Shannon", I think, was with my father, who was taking me to London en route to school, and I remember how we were dug out of snowdrifts and had to follow snowploughs in many places. We arrived at the White Horse, Ipswich, very late, and could not go on to London that day.

William Edgell, Letter (1926) to *East Anglian Daily Times*

30. ON THE MOVE – III

I can't omit, however little it may seem, that this county of Suffolk is particularly famous for furnishing the city of London and all the counties round, with turkeys; and 'tis thought, there are more turkeys bred in this county, and the part of Norfolk that adjoins to it, than in all the rest of England, especially for sale; tho' this may be reckoned, as I say above, but a trifling thing to take notice of in these remarks; yet, as I have hinted, that I shall observe, how London is in general supplied with all its provisions from the whole body of the nation, and how every part of the island is engaged in some degree or other of that supply; On this account I could not omit it; nor will it be found so inconsiderable an article as some may imagin, if this be true which I receiv'd an account of from a person living on the place, (viz.) That they have counted 300 droves of turkeys (for they drive them all in droves on foot) pass in one season over Stratford-Bridge on the River Stour, which parts Suffolk from Essex, about six miles from Colchester on the road from Ipswich to London. These droves, as they say, generally contain from three hundred to a thousand each drove; so that one may suppose them to contain 500 one with another, which is 150,000 in all; and yet this is one of the least passages, the numbers which travel by New Market-Heath, and the open country and the forest, and also the numbers that come by Sudbury and Clare, being many more.

For the further supplies of the markets of London with poultry, of which these countries particularly abound; they have within these few years found it practicable to make the geese travel on foot too, as well as the turkeys; and a prodigious number are brought up to London in droves from the farthest parts of Norfolk; even from the fenn-country, about Lynn, Downham, Wisbich, and the Washes; as also from all the east side of Norfolk and Suffolk, of whom 'tis very frequent now to meet droves, with a thousand, sometimes two thousand in a drove: They begin to drive them generally in August, by which time the harvest is almost over, and the geese may feed in the stubbles as they go. Thus they hold on to the end of October, when the roads begin to be too stiff and deep for their broad feet and short leggs to march in.

Daniel Defoe, *A Tour Through the Whole Island of Great Britain*

31. ON THE MOVE – IV

(See no 7 in this section.)

For my own part, my occupation in my solitary pilgrimages was to recall every yard of the old road as I went along it, and to haunt the old spots, of which I never tired. I haunted them, as my memory had often done, and lingered among them as my younger thoughts had lingered when I was far away. The grave beneath the tree, where both my parents lay – on which I had looked out, when it was my father's only, with such curious feelings of compassion, and by which I had stood, so desolate, when it was opened to receive my pretty mother and her baby – the grave which Peggotty's own faithful care had ever since kept neat, and made a garden of, I walked near, by the hour. It lay a little off the churchyard path, in a quiet corner, not so far removed but I could read the names upon the stone as I walked to and fro, startled by the sound of the church-bell when it struck the hour, for it was like a departed voice to me . . .

There were great changes in my old home. The ragged nests, so long deserted by the rooks, were gone; and the trees were lopped and topped out of their remembered shapes. The garden had run wild, and half the windows of the house were shut up. It was occupied, but only by a poor lunatic gentleman, and the people who took care of him. He was always sitting at my little window, looking out into the churchyard; and I wondered whether his rambling thoughts ever went upon any of the fancies that used to occupy mine, on the rosy mornings when I peeped out of that same little window in my night-clothes, and saw the sheep quietly feeding in the light of the rising sun.

Charles Dickens, *David Copperfield*

32. ON THE MOVE – V

I alighted from the dinghy at a landing-stage which seemed in direct line for Levington; it led immediately into Orwell Park. I have found the landowners in this district agreeably lenient to the trespasser. "There are trespassers and trespassers," as a certain gamekeeper told me. I hope I shall always be one of those who receive a nod and a wink.

I do not think I have ever seen deer with quite such varied colouring as those who live in Orwell Park. I thought at first these were part of the undergrowth and the first sign of an early autumn. They clustered, in colourful bunches of fawn, brown, and red, among the ferns and in the shadows under the trees, but they broke to life at the sound of the trespasser's footfall, startling me as I had startled them. The park, rich in splendid trees, led to the house. There is something to be said for knocking at a door if one desires to enter, I have rarely found entrance denied, though this is more certain in the cottage than the castle; but Orwell Park graciously opened its doors and displayed its treasures to the stranger within its gates. I found the house as rich in works of art as the park was in trees – Gainsborough, Van Ostade, A. Cuyp, Jan Steen, Van der Neer,

Vandyck, Holbein, Murillo, Andrea del Sarto, and Titian. Murillo's celebrated picture of Christ healing the lame man at the Pool of Bethseda is
here, considered by many to be his finest picture . . . but today the earth
was superbly painted with a master brush, and the greatest human effort
could not hold me from contemplation of the Divine Artist's work.

When I left I walked decorously down the drive until I felt the house
had lost interest in me, then I struck off and climbed the fence which
divided the Orwell Estate from the Broke Hall Estate, and proceeded with
my incorrigible trespassing through the Nacton woods. The sun was
strong and the shadows cool and deep. A wood companioned with water
brings rest and entertainment to the weary mortal; it is full of music,
particularly on a day such as this, when the water tumbles and laughs as it
washes the varied fringe of the wood's skirt. Above, about, and around
there is a stir and a rustling, and, for most of the year, a chorus of birds.
There are days when all the world sparkles and dances, and this was one
of them.

Nancy Price, *The Gull's Way*

33. ON THE MOVE – VI

The walks and drives in the neighbourhood are diversified and pleasing;
and whether the romantic vicinities of the lake or the woodland glades
and sylvan scenery found towards Somerleyton be chosen, the rambler
will find his attention equally attracted by the numerous objects for contemplation profusely scattered around. The lover of nature will meet
spots where imagination may indulge in her –

> *Airy mood*
> *To every murmur of the wood;*
> *The bee in yonder flowery nook,*
> *The chidings of the headlong brook;*
> *The green leaf shivering in the gale,*
> *The warbling hill, the lowing vale.*

The extreme beauty and luxuriance of English rural scenery has ever
been a favourite theme of our descriptive writers and poets, and has been
especially celebrated by the Suffolk poets, Crabbe and Bloomfield. It is
moreover, one of those national features of which an Englishman may
well be proud, because of the efforts of his countreymen in aid of the
bounty of nature, for much of the beauty of our rural scenery is owing to
the high state of cultivation to which the land has been brought and the
consequent fertility that is the prominent feature of all English landscapes, although irrespective of that trait, perhaps no other country can

present such an extent and diversity of views, undulating plains, swelling heights, grassy nooks and sparkling rivulets.

And for this rustic order of landscape, presenting "Nature's silent fingering," Suffolk is unsurpassed, more especially in this corner of the county named Lothingland. In a district where the walks or drives are so numerous and all so beautiful, It would be almost capricious to point out any as being entitled to pre-eminence. Nevertheless, we shall endeavour to describe a few spots, with some slight minutiae regarding some objects of interest. A walk of about a mile from the town brings us into a lane leading to Mutford Bridge, where an artificial embankment divides Lake Lothing into two portions, the inner one being named Oulton Broad, full of fresh water, the flood-gates separating it from the salt on the side next the sea.

Should the pedestrian still wish to continue his walk, a delightful one will take him to Oulton, along a line of peculiar verdure and loveliness. The hedges here exhale delicious fragrance, composed as they are of sweet briar, eglantine, and hawthorn, the wild rose, though scentless, adding much to the beauty of their appearance. Beneath the banks "many a garden flower grows wild," the hyacinth, the violet, and the mignonette lending their perfumes to regale the senses of the wanderer. Nearly all the lanes of this vicinity abound with beautiful strips of heath, overhung with the yellow-flowered gorse.

A. D. Bayne, *The Illustrated History of Eastern England*

34. ON THE MOVE – VII

I followed her suggestion and found a lovely walk along the Stour, with the light dying in the sky and the moon beginning to shine. There were tall poplars along the stream, and the air was fragrant with flowers and the evening mist. I returned to my room and slept soundly, fatigued by the longest bit of cycling I had done yet.

The next day was bright and crisp and clear, and I awoke with the sun streaming into the room. For breakfast I had two more fresh eggs and my hostess showed me her trim little garden, already bright with spring flowers, and the poultry run, whence came the eggs I had so much enjoyed.

After breakfast I took a walk about the town and visited the church, a fourteenth century building. In the north aisle is a delightful monument to a seventeenth century dignitary and his wife, who kneel facing each other, with their six sons and eight daughters kneeling below them, arranged stair-step-wise.

Then I started for Nayland, through the fresh spring morning, along the valley of the Stour. This is the country that Constable loved and painted, and each turn in the road brought into view a scene reminiscent of his canvases.

Nayland was ablaze with wistaria, a gem of a village, quiet, clean, and smiling in the sun.

John T. Appleby, *Suffolk Summer*

35. A View Confirmed

We found that the scenery of eight or ten of our late friend's most important subjects might be enclosed by a circle of a few hundred yards at Flatford, very near Bergholt; within this space are the lock, which forms the subject of several pictures – Willy Lott's House – the little raised wooden bridge and the picturesque cottage near it, seen in the picture engraved for Messrs. Finden's work ('View on the Stour'), and introduced into others – and the meadow in which the picture of 'Boatbuilding' was entirely painted. So startling was the resemblance of some of these scenes to the pictures of them, which we knew so well, that we could hardly believe we were for the first time standing on the ground from which they were painted. Of others, we found that Constable had rather combined and varied the materials, than given exact views.

C. R. Leslie, *Life of Constable*

36. On the Move – VIII

It was a misty mid-January afternoon when Everard started out for his first walk along the Boxford road. It was freezing hard, although little rime was to be seen on the grass-stalks, freezing with a dull, pitiless cold that sank into the flesh and numbed it. This mist hung like a colourless fleece, quenching all shape but the black outline of adjacent hedges; the road rang flat and meaningless to the foot like a counterfeit coin; all nature was lifeless and only the elm-trees, their frozen twigs a maze of ghostly filigree, were beautiful. It was not a propitious afternoon for a walk, but Everard, having been twice thwarted by circumstance – in the form of rain and an invitation to tea at the Vale Farm – was only the more set on seizing the first opportunity that offered. There was something quite peculiar in the singleness and insistence of his desire to meet Ruthie Gathercole. He had not once questioned its prudence nor debated its genuineness; to nothing in his life was it comparable except the undeniable urge which had brought him to Lindmer; to feel it was to obey. The disappointments of the two previous Sundays had only goaded him further, and although he would have been more comfortable in front of his

sitting-room fire, or more usefully occupied laying out his neglected par-
terre, he doggedly turned his face to the road.

The road was deserted – even the village street had been empty, except
for a little boy at a gate who had stared and said hullo – and the fear
crossed Everard that perhaps Ruthie Gathercole, too, would prefer an
afternoon by the fire to a drive in such bleak, forbidding weather. If she
came, at least they would have the road to themselves. A startled bird fled
at his approach, as if it were ashamed to be seen on such a day, and the
whir of its wings was an outrage to his ear, straining for the sound of
hoofs. A mile further on he stopped to listen. There was a faint sound in
the depths of the mist, at first like the muffled tap of a distant wood-
pecker, and then gradually resolving itself into the loose rhythm of a slow-
trotting pony, followed by the rasp and rattle of iron-tyred cartwheels. He
peered into the greyness but could see nothing: nor could she, if it were
she, until she was almost on top of him, but the sudden recognition would
be less embarrassing than sighting each other at a distance. The sound of
wheels and the stroke of hoofs merged into one confused clatter, and a high
dogcart rolled out of the mist into view. Everard's heart beat hard. The
driver lolling on the high seat was a woman, and he recognised her as
Ruthie Gathercole more by her height and build than anything else, for
he had never seen her in a hat before. At the sight of a pedestrian she drew
off the crown of the road towards the hedgerow and as she came level,
Everard looked up and raised his hat.

'Good afternoon, Miss Gathercole,' he said.

She stared down hard at him as she passed, and recognised him with a
start. She fumbled hesitantly with the reins for a moment, and then
pulled up sharply a few yards ahead of him.

'Why, who'd have thought of seeing you here, Mr. Mulliver?'

'Or you?'

Neither deceived the other, but politeness was satisfied.

'Are you going to Boxford, Mr. Mulliver?' she asked gravely.

'I thought of going that way,' he replied with equal gravity.

'Can I give you a lift?' she said, symbolically shifting to the end of her
high seat.

'Thank you, I'd be glad,' he answered, doing his best to keep the
eagerness out of his voice, but succeeding ill.

He climbed hastily into the trap and swayed down beside her as the
pony ambled off. She did not trouble to urge it into a trot, and for some
minutes they watched the rise and fall of its quarters, tongue-tied and
abashed with their proximity. Then, as on the brink of blushing,
Everard's cheeks began to tingle; he could feel her eyes upon his face,
furtively scanning its details – the square chin, full lips and long, straight
nose, the calm, high forehead over wide-set, still, dark-blue eyes. He went
on desperately gazing at the pony's quarters, his heart thumping louder

every second, and he would have blushed outright if she had not broken the silence. It was a relief to have an excuse for looking at her.

'What brought you out on an afternoon like this, Mr. Mulliver?'

He shrugged his shoulders.

'I just came out for a walk,' he said nonchalantly. 'And you?'

'I always come this way,' she replied.

'Did you come this way last Sunday?' It was an unnecessary question.

'Yes, and you went to Vale Farm,' she answered, as if to justify it.

'How did you know that?' he asked quickly.

'I saw you from our window after I came back,' she replied, idly tugging at the lash of her whip. 'We can see right down to the bottom of the valley. It was wet the Sunday before,' she added irrelevantly, but not without understanding.

'Yes, it was,' said Everard thoughtfully.

H. W. Freeman, *Down in the Valley*

37. ON THE MOVE – IX

In passing we saw an estate which belonged to one of our Bury friends, who has now sold it. Only a house is wanting to make it a very pleasant place; the stretch of water, which is vast, looks like a natural river. The name of the place is Holbrook. A little further on is Woolverston, which belongs to Mr. Berners. A short time ago he built quite a good house there in modern style. However, the whole merit of the house lies in its site; it stands on the top of a hill, in the middle of a vast, ill-kept park. The estate consists simply of a wide expanse of enclosed land covered with turf and trees and lacking in any proper design. No care has been taken to devise elegant points of view; in a word, it is such as Nature has willed.

The position of the house is very attractive in that one gets a view over the tops of the trees which cover the slope of the hill, or the river at Ipswich, which is about three-quarters of a mile wide and which forms a crescent round the park; through the branches of the same trees you may see the water which washes their feet, and in certain places where the trees are taller it appears as though there is no water between you and the opposite shore. At the foot of the picture is the town of Ipswich, which rounds it off splendidly, though it is at a distance which prevents one from distinguishing individual objects.

The large number of small vessels with which the river is always covered adds an element of life to this superb view, but it seems to me a pity that one should see it all at once and in a single glance. The view is truly grand only from the second floor of the house; from the first floor one does not see enough.

As soon as we had seen the house and park, we got on the road again for Ipswich, continuing to follow the line of the river, or rather of the bay. You pass through another village, and the road is pleasant the whole way. Ipswich is situated at the foot of the bay, as it is at about this point that the tide ceases to make itself appreciably felt.

François de la Rochefoucauld, *A Frenchman in England*

38. ON THE MOVE – X

The journey described in the following extract is one from Eatanswill (Sudbury) to Bury St. Edmunds.

By that time, Mr. Pickwick and Sam Weller, perched on the outside of a stage coach, were every succeeding minute placing a less and less distance between themselves and the good old town of Bury St. Edmunds.

$$* \qquad * \qquad *$$

There is no month in the whole year, in which nature wears a more beautiful appearance than in the month of August. Spring has many beauties, and May is a fresh and blooming month, but the charms of this time of year are enhanced by their contrast with the winter season. August has no such advantage. It comes when we remember nothing but clear skies, green fields and sweet-smelling flowers – when the recollection of snow, and ice, and bleak winds, has faded from our minds as completely as they have disappeared from the earth, – and yet what a pleasant time it is! Orchards and corn-fields ring with the hum of labour; trees bend beneath the thick clusters of rich fruit which bow their branches to the ground; and the corn, piled in graceful sheaves, or waving in every light breath that sweeps above it, as if it wooed the sickle, tinges the landscape with a golden hue. A mellow softness appears to hang over the whole earth; the influence of the season seems to extend itself to the very waggon, whose slow motion across the well-reaped field, is perceptible only to the eye, but strikes with no harsh sound upon the ear.

As the coach rolls swiftly past the fields and orchards which skirt the road, groups of women and children, piling the fruit in sieves, or gathering the scattered ears of corn, pause for an instant from their labour, and shading the sun-burnt face with a still browner hand, gaze upon the passengers with curious eyes, while some stout urchin, too small to work, but too mischievous to be left at home, scrambles over the side of the basket in which he has been deposited for security, and kicks and screams with delight. The reaper stops in his work, and stands with folded arms, looking at the vehicle as it whirls past; and the rough cart-horses bestow a sleepy glance upon the smart coach team, which says, as plainly as a horse's glance can, 'It's all very fine to look at, but slow going, over a heavy field, is better than warm work like that, upon a dusty road, after all.' You cast a look behind you, as you turn a corner of the road. The women and children have resumed their labour: the reaper once more stoops to his work: the cart-horses have moved on: and all are again in motion.

Charles Dickens, *The Pickwick Papers*

39. THE FRONT DOOR

Off to the left hand, in strong contrast with this level stretch of road, the country is tumbled into combes and rounded hills, where the River Gipping takes its rise in the village of that name, springing from the hill where the church tower stands solemn and grim, as though it held inviolate the story of the place, away from those days when the Gippings first settled here and gave it a title.

But let not the hurried seek Gipping, along the winding by-roads. The way, if not far, is not easy, and passengers are few. Scattered and infrequent farmhouses there be, at whose back doors to inquire the way, but rustic directions are apt to mislead. In any case, it is little use approaching the front door of a farmhouse. No one will hear you knocking, unless indeed it be a watchful and savage dog, trained to be on the alert for tramps; and you are like to hear him snuffling and gasping on the other side in a ferociously suggestive manner which will render you thankful that the door is closed and bolted. And not only bolted on this occasion, but always. The steps, and the space between the door and the threshold, where stray straws and wind-blown rubbish have collected, are evidence of the fact that the farmer and his family do not use the front door, but make their exits and entrances by way of the kitchen. It is an old East Anglian custom, and although many of the farmers nowadays pretend to culture and set up to be as up-to-date as the retired tradesfolk and small squires they are neighbourly with, many others would no more think of using the principal entrance to their homes than they would make use of the "parlour", where massive and sombre furniture, covered with antimacassars, is disposed with geometric accuracy around the room, in company with the family Bible and the prizes taken at school by the farmer's children; the stale and stuffy atmosphere proclaiming that this state apartment is only used on rare and solemn occasions. In fact, the "best room" and the front door only came into use in the old days on the occasion of a funeral. Perhaps it is a custom originating in a laudable idea of paying the greatest possible respect to the dead, but it is one which certainly gives a gruesome mortuary significance to both the entrance and the room.

CHARLES HARPER, *The Norwich Road*

40. THE POSTMAN FROM BENFIELD

"The post," he said, "was brought out from Sudbury by cart in them days; and at the time I'm tellin' you of, the job was contracted out to a man that lived over at Benfield. He drove a little closed-in box of a cart, on high wheels, with painted spokes nigh as thin as matches. A mule drew the cart and sometimes you'd meet it fair flyin' along the roads. On the way back to Sudbury each night, the postman – he wore a little ol' pill-box hat, I remember – used to call at Larkfield, Shepfield and Stalling to pick up the mail-bags. There he sat, perched up on top of his little red cart, in a sort of fenced-in seat. The mail-box was padlocked at the back; and each post-master – or whatever you like to call 'em, for mostly they did a dozen other jobs besides – had his own key. He'd hurry out with the mail-bag, unlock the box, fling the bag in, and then lock it up again. "Night, Joe," he'd say; and without so much as a word from the driver, or a flick o' the whip, away that ol' mule 'ld goo like a streak of lightnin'. He knew the roads just as well as Joe himself did.

"Well, we used to have rare hard winter weather then – sometimes it 'ld be below zero. More'n once I've played games on the pond when I was a kid: bowlin' for oranges instead of coconuts, you know. Why, the water would be frozen so thick that even the ground underneath was frozen too. But as I was sayin', there'd be ol' Joe, sittin' up there on his high seat, all muffled up to the ears so's you couldn't tell whether he answered you or not. And one mighty cold night, he came rattlin' along the road same as usual, and called at all the post-offices like he did every blessed night of the year. It was so cold that whenever he stopped, the postmaster just flung the mail-bag into the back of the cart, locked up the box as quick as ever he could, and scuttled off indoors again out of the weather. 'Night, Joe!' he called, and away went the mule. When they got to Sudbury, they pulled into the post-office yard, and somebody came out to collect the bags. 'You've had a cold ride tonight, Joe, and no mistake,' he said. But Joe never answered a word. He just sat up there on his perch, without so much as movin' a hand – for he was frozen dead in his seat. And nobody ever knowed whereabouts on the road it happened."

C. HENRY WARREN, *Happy Countryman*

41. THE GREATCOAT

Among the most quaint and interesting people in the parish was John Brady. He could hardly have come from the East Anglian stock. Slight in figure and quick in movement, with curly black hair and shaggy eyebrows shading his poor defective eyes, he bore no resemblance to the fair-haired, blue-eyed type so usual in Suffolk. John was musical and played the fiddle, he also had a fine voice, and at one time was in request at the public-houses in the evenings. His music and songs attracted visitors and helped the sale of beer. But he was a religious man and knew that this occupation was a dangerous one for himself as well as the reverse of useful to other people. He resolved to abandon his musical evenings at the public-houses, even though this entailed much hardship and loss of money. How he managed to live I cannot say, for he could not work at a trade and was not strong enough for field labour. Sometimes he purchased salt herrings and walked for miles to the small villages with his basket to sell them. Sometimes he carried messages, and I think kind people gave him occasional assistance. Somehow he did rub along.

One snowy night my father came into the house without his greatcoat but with flakes of snow adhering to his clothes. 'What have you done with your coat?' asked my mother. 'Well,' he said, 'I met poor John Brady and he had such a thin suit and it was white with snow so I gave him my coat.' 'That is good,' said mother, 'now you must buy yourself a new one.' There was little money to spare at the Vicarage, and my father clung to his old garments with a tenacity which his good wife thought was carried to an extreme.

Many years afterwards my brother Vaughan and I revisited Debenham, and when driving from Needham station, Andrews, the man from the Inn who had met us with a dogcart, said, 'There is old John Brady on ahead; we must give him a call.' 'John, John, I have got Mr. James and Mr. Vaughan here,' he called as we drew level with the little pony cart Brady was driving. Times were better with him now and he had a conveyance. Brady pulled up, placed the reins on the seat (his little dog at once put his paws on them lest they should fall by the pony's feet), and hurried across the road to greet us. Then he ran back and fetched from the cart a folded garment more green than black. 'There, do you know that?' and we did. There was no mistaking its length and one-time respectability. 'That was your father's coat which he took off his own shoulders and put onto mine one snowy night. It has got thin now, but if it don't allers warm the body it never fail to warm the heart.'

James Cornish, *Reminiscences of Country Life*

42. FARMING IN THE 1860s AND THE HORSE

My father, Charles John Cornish, was Vicar of Debenham in Suffolk from 1860 to 1883. It was a large village of more than a thousand people, and as the villages for nearly eight miles round were much smaller, Debenham formed a centre of some importance. It lies in the middle of a great stretch of heavy clay land; in fact, for ten miles to the east and west, and for fifteen miles to the north and south, there is scarcely an acre of light land.

The clay, though somewhat sticky, produced wonderful crops of corn, beans and mangold. It may have been largely because the country was not very attractive for residents that over this great area the houses of country gentry were scarce. There were two or three great houses, the finest of them being Helmingham Hall, with its deer park and splendid old oaks and herd of red deer, but in almost all the villages the aristocracy consisted of the farmers and the parson. The intensity of cultivation undoubtedly diminished the picturesqueness of the country. One hardly ever saw an acre of land that was not cultivated; few woods, and no heaths or other wild country. The yield of the land was prodigious. In many parts of England only a small percentage of the acres in the parish produce much food, but at Debenham I think that some two acres of village green and less than that area of wayside strips were the only spaces that were not so utilised. And what prosperity there was for the farmers and land-owners, though, alas, not for the workers on the land! The amount of efficient labour at the disposal of the farmers was practically unlimited. I well remember the gangs of children, boys and girls, at work in the fields, picking up stones to mend the roads, or dropping beans. For this a man would walk backwards with a heavy dibble in each hand, making a couple of holes at each pace, and the children would follow him, dropping a bean in each hole. The method by which the stones were utilised for mending the roads was very simple. When winter came they were taken from the stone heaps at the road side and spread where the ruts were deepest. There they remained loose until gradually worn in by the wheeled traffic.

The gang system led to so many dreadful results that it was prohibited by Act of Parliament. The farm labourers were paid a very small wage, and the housing conditions were deplorably bad.

With abundant cheap labour the standard of farming was remarkably high. The horses, the famous Suffolk punches, were excellent. Their fetlocks free from hair were well adapted for work on the heavy soil; their short legs, long, powerful bodies and high courage made them well qualified for full days of ploughing in a stiff soil. It was beautiful to see five or six pairs at work breaking the stubble on a fine autumn morning, their chestnut coats glistening in the sun.

James Cornish, *Reminiscences of Country Life*

43. The Horse

Among the many ornaments of this shire, I may not omitt to speake here of the horse, for the breeding whereof this country hath many apt places of most profitable use, wherein some chuse the low and fruitfull grounds, the fertility of which soile being a rich black mould, they deem most fitt for these purposes; butt experience teacheth that the low grounds seldome or never do afford a strong colt for service, or of quick life or spirritt, butt onely such as are fitt for burden and draught, the better sort for their breed as nere as they can well make choice of is knowls or the height of hills, where good ground is with plenty of pasture, from whence they find that because of the aire above is there alwaies fresh, pure, and transparent, and the soile beneathe is firme and almost stony, the colt here bred is most puissant, and strong for service, of quick life, and spirritt, of high pride, and most comely shape . . . And of those I have seen some coming over beyond sea, have been admired for their painfull travell in long journies, their firme carriage in time of service, their quicknes, and readines in all necessities, butt of all for their continuance in time of battle, never giving in, butt when other the choicest of all other countries, especially if the march have bin any thing long, or the skirmish any thing hott, have soon fainted, and tyred; these have been still noted to bee yett most fresh, carrying their riders with nott a little creditt, and estimation, which if it were of our better sort here well weighed, would encourage every man to breed, and having bred to make much of so special a worth which every country cannot speake of . . .

Richard Ryece, *The Breviary of Suffolk*

44. AND ITS USE

"One day, whilst in trouble, I was visited by a person I had occasionally met at sporting dinners. He came to look after a Suffolk Punch, the best horse, by the bye, that anybody can purchase to drive, it being the only animal of the horse kind in England that will pull twice at a dead weight. I told him that I had none at that time that I could recommend; in fact, that every horse in my stable was sick. He then invited me to dine with him at an inn close by, and I was glad to go with him, in the hope of getting rid of unpleasant thoughts. After dinner, during which he talked nothing but slang, observing I looked very melancholy, he asked me what was the matter with me, and I, my heart being opened by the wine he had made me drink, told him my circumstances without reserve. With an oath or two for not having treated him at first like a friend, he said he would soon set me all right; and pulling out two hundred pounds, told me to pay him when I could. I felt as I never felt before; however, I took his notes, paid my sneaks, and in less than three months was right again, and had returned him his money. On paying it to him, I said that I now had a Punch which would just suit him, saying that I would give it to him – a free gift – for nothing. He swore at me; telling me to keep my Punch, for that he was suited already. I begged him to tell me how I could requite him for his kindness, whereupon, with the most dreadful oath I ever heard, he bade me come and see him hanged when his time was come. I wrung his hand, and told him I would, and I kept my word. The night before the day he was hanged at H--, I harnessed a Suffolk Punch to my light gig, the same Punch which I had offered to him, which I have ever since kept, and which brought me and this short young man to Horncastle, and in eleven hours I drove that Punch one hundred and ten miles. I arrived at H-- just in the nick of time. There was the ugly jail – the scaffold – and there upon it stood the only friend I had ever had in the world. Driving my Punch, which was all in a foam, into the midst of the crowd, which made way for me as if it knew what I came for, I stood up in my gig, took off my hat, and shouted, 'God Almighty bless you, Jack!' The dying man turned his pale grim face towards me – for his face was always somewhat grim, do you see – nodded, and said, or I thought I heard him say, 'All right, old chap.' The next moment – my eyes water.

George Borrow, *The Romany Rye*

45. THE DRY

Just out of sight over the crest of the park's gentle hill, harvest is in full swing: and just out of sight to east, west and north also, hidden from us by trees. Our shallow tree-fringed dell is loud with the noise of it – binders clack, tractors snarl, cough and break into their continuous roar, and the combine harvester makes a bourdon to it all like the deep buzzing of a giant bumble-bee. But unless we choose to breast the hill, we see none of it. Within the dell, there is complete idleness. Harry has been taken away from the garden to help in the fields, and I am idle, except for the odd job of seed-collecting, or cutting down dead things. There is nothing much one can do, in such a state of drought.

I came back from the sea to find all the summer flowers dried up and dead, except the upper blooms of the hollyhocks, so I spent a few days in clearance. That was at the beginning of the month. The drought was so intense that I feared for the life of the Michaelmas daisies, which, though hardy, are shallow-rooted. However, there was a good thunderstorm just in time to save them, after which the drought set in again. And as a farmer's wife I ought to be glad of it. A single storm and a quick dry afterwards does not hurt the harvest, unless the rain should happen to come on a strong wind, but prolonged rain, or showery weather, or a series of storms are very undesirable. Ripe corn which is continually wet-and-dry is liable to begin to grow as it stands in the stook. No danger of that this year. (Or ought I to cross my fingers? The harvest is so heavy that it may run on into September, and who knows what may happen in our delightful climate, which gives us so few long "settled" periods.)

Strange that the corn should be so well-eared, and the early-sown stuff so tall in the straw besides, when my poor old garden has had to be kept going with the washing-up water. The Master says no farmer in these parts ever yet went broke through drought, though wet years have seen the end of many. I can only conclude that this house and garden stand upon the sandy high-water mark of pre-historic floods; the rising ground to the south is quite good land which stands a dry season, and the valley bottom to the north (perhaps a foot lower in altitude than the garden) is nice, rich, black soil. It is very bad luck to be a gardener on the sandy belt, and to see everything flourishing, rain or no rain, on either hand, while one's loved and hand-raised plants shrivel and die.

Doreen Wallace, *In a Green Shade*

46. The Dry, and Wild Plants

A countryside as arid and sandy as ours cannot expect to be remarkable for its wild flowers. Yet those we have go far to make up for what we lose in variety. I am no botanist, I am afraid; and I look on wild flowers with a gardener's eye.

Down by the stream the king-cups are the first flowers, a welcome gold near the catkinned willows and alders warming the heart under a too frequently icy April sky. One associates them with drumming snipe and squealing peewits. Later comes the water forget-me-not which in places covers the edges of the stream with a pale blue haze. And at this season, too, the yellow flags, most graceful of water plants, make a lovely picture.

Near the stream, again, you will find huge patches of meadowsweet, delicious in scent as it is charming to the eye. Your legs, brushing wild mint, fill the air with fragrance. And in the more open, damper places are the early purple and bog orchises, where presently there will be ragged robin and the small, dark blue scabious.

We are too dry and limeless for many of the orchis family. The only other that I can think of is the lesser twayblade which grows in a boggy, shady place. And I have very occasionally found lady's tresses in late summer.

The chief glories of our summer are, however, the wild roses and the honeysuckle. I have written elsewhere that, to my eye, the dog rose seems to flower more wonderfully in East Anglia than anywhere else in England. Certainly a Suffolk hedgerow full of honeysuckle and dog roses is hard to beat in Nature.

I have mentioned already that the honeysuckle grows abundantly in the Forest. There is a peculiarly sensuous pleasure in walking there on a summer evening suddenly to meet a wave of unexpected fragrance from a honeysuckle hidden round a corner.

Down stream, at a place delightfully named Padley Water, there is something very special. I had heard of it from Mr. Goodheart, and bicycled off that very afternoon. At the nearest cottage I asked a woman if this were the right place. "Yes, that's Padley Water across the field. But I've never been down to see them myself." She lived within two hundred yards of the water-lilies! Perhaps such bucolic indifference accounts for the survival of many of our country flowers.

Yes, there they were, dozens of creamy white water-lilies with golden centres, the only wild ones of their kind for perhaps twenty miles around. They are almost the most beautiful, certainly the largest, British flower. And long may they be preserved at Padley Water.

Hugh Farmar, *The Cottage in the Forest*

The following – not entirely accurate – description of a fascinating stretch of coastline is included for its vivid imaginative qualities.

47. ALONG THE COAST

With the passing of the Dunwich headland the stream, sweeping close inshore where formerly a bay had been, began to move the coast bodily southward. The Alde, running straight into the sea, began to move as well, the shingle piling up gradually, inexorably forcing the river sideways. So the little town of Orford saw a waterway coming to it, saw it draw level and watched it pass, leaving it on the side of a river. As it crept along, grasses began to grow, solidifying and consolidating the shingle into firm ground, firm enough to support the lighthouse erected upon it. It crept onwards six miles beyond Orford before it allowed the river to enter the sea at Shingle Street. Or rather, *below* Shingle Street, because it is within living memory that the Ore's mouth was two miles further south.

Shingle Street! A queer, outlandish, savage place, inhospitable and bare. The motorist jogging along comfortably and pleasantly from Woodbridge will find his lovely Suffolk lanes giving place to flat, less wooded country; as he goes he will begin to notice deep ditches and waterways following the road on either side, until at length a great wall of shingle confronts him. Shingle Street! Through a dip the road leads to where the old 'Life Boat Inn' stood with a cluster of houses ranging on either side, flanked in turn by Martello towers. The charming little village had to be evacuated during the war, was used as a target, and blown to pieces.

When the river passed the inn, flowing out to sea below the Martello tower, old inhabitants will tell you how large brigs came in loaded with timber to discharge at the quay abreast the 'Life Boat'. It was a busy place then and prosperous. Today no vessels lie securely guarded from the sea by a shingle bank; today nothing is left but large deep ponds between the houses and the sea to show where the river once ran.

Sometimes a dinghy or two are pushed over the yielding shingle and set afloat to do a little fishing, but that is all. Only the stones are left, moved ceaselessly by the eternal swell which, falls it never so lazily upon the beach, yet draws a harsh grating note from the shingle it undermines and sucks to seaward on the ebb or heaps up on the flood.

That beach is never still, is never silent.

Two miles north, marked by coastguard houses on shore and a smother of white tormented foam at sea, lies the entrance to the Ore. Coarse binding grasses on the brow make for slightly easier walking than on the yielding shingle below. Here the beautiful pale yellow flowers and large handsome green leaves of the handsome sea poppy flourish, three feet high. You may find also the creeping sea pea. Its purple blossoms are rare in England, being seen only, so I am told, along this little stretch of Suffolk coast. The two beacons ashore, moved as occasion demands, are the only marks to assist the mariner. To seaward there are no marks at all.

At high water with the current in a state of suspended animation it looks guileless. At the turn of the tide things begin to happen. After high water it is only a matter of minutes before the ebb attains a velocity great enough to prevent any but powerfully engined vessels from making head-way. In all directions humps of shingle appear, growing larger, higher and more awe-inspiring as the tide-level falls, until at low water the entire entrance becomes an extensive mass, half water, half shingle. The mounds take upon themselves fantastic shapes. That seven-knot run of tide scours away their sides-forming beautiful easy, flowing curves. Some rise up fashioned like embattled towers perched on steep-to cliffs admirable for defence, others sprawl across the entrance resembling gigantic sea mon-sters half submerged and sleeping. Vast lakes containing small fish are fashioned. As the watcher sitting on the mainland surveys the scene before him, when all, as he thinks, is quiet at near low water, suddenly a castle, becoming top heavy, falls over with a roar and causes a few startled gulls to add to the momentary pandemonium. The last of the ebb slips out, still, however, running fast for an East Coast river, taking with it, perhaps, a treasured doll left on the tide-line by some careless child at Snape Bridge fifteen miles inland.

Archie White, *Tideways and Byways of Essex and Suffolk*

48. THE SAME, FROM THE SEA

"I don't see any islands," said Bridget.

"Right ahead of us," said Daddy.

Ahead of them the land seemed hardly above the level of the sea, just a long low line above the water, with higher ground far away behind it. But that low line of coast seemed to have no gaps in it. It looked as if it stretched the whole way round across the head of the bay. Even John began to doubt if there could be islands ahead. But Daddy was ticking off one buoy after another on Jim's chart and seemed quite sure of his way. A couple of men were hauling a trawl net in a small boat and a cloud of gulls hovered above them. A motor boat appeared ahead, came to meet them and passed them in a flurry of foam.

"She must have come out from somewhere," said Titty, but still could see no gap in the coast line.

"We're nearly there," said Daddy at last. "Look out for a round buoy with a cross on a stick above it.'

"There is is," called John. "Close to the shore."

Almost at the same moment, everybody saw a break in the line of sand away to the south, and a thread of water going in there, and one or two tall masts showing above sand dunes. And, as they came nearer to that round buoy with the cross they saw that a much wider channel was opening before them with smooth shining water stretching to the west and low banks on either side.

"There you are," said Daddy. "That buoy marks the cross roads. Turn left, follow that creek in there, past those masts, and you'll come to a town."

"I can see houses now," said Roger, "and lots more boats."

"You can get right up to the town at high water in a dinghy. But if you go, don't wait there too long, or there won't be water to take you back."

"But we're going to an island aren't we?" said Titty. "Not a town."

"We are," said Daddy. "We leave that buoy to port and carry straight on."

"Crossroads buoy," said Roger as they passed it.

A minute or two later they had left the open bay and the *Goblin* was slipping easily along in the quiet water of an inland sea. A low spit of land with a dyke along it already hid the creek that led to the town, though they could still see the tops of distant masts. Far away, on the opposite side, was another low dyke. Standing on the deck and in the cockpit they could see bushes here and there. Ahead of them the inland sea seemed to stretch on for ever.

"What's it called," asked Titty, from the foredeck.

Daddy smiled. "Do you want the name on Jim's chart? I thought you'd give it a name yourselves."

"It's a very secret place," said Roger. "You don't see it until you're almost inside."

"Secret Water," said Titty. "Let's call it that."

Arthur Ransome, *Secret Water*

49. A NOTE FROM A CELLO

*In the summer of 1969 the Maltings, the great concert-hall near Aldeburgh,
was destroyed by fire. These lines were written to celebrate its restoration in
1970.*

> *A blameless calm night, the people have gone.*
> *Dark thickets of reeds feel a breath of disquiet:*
> *Moorhens awake; fear saves the vole*
> *About to be hooked by the soft-flying owl;*
> *In the marshes of Snape a sluice and a pool*
> *Make suddenly shapes of flame-coloured light.*
>
> *A crackle of fire! An undeclared war,*
> *Motiveless, strives at those who contrived*
> *That resonant shell, at ears that have heard*
> *Rejoicings derived, in nights darker by far,*
> *From far greater fires, wells deeper, deep dreams,*
> *Granite, violets, blood, the pureness of dew.*
>
> *The shell is restored. The orchestra settles.*
> *A baton is raised. Renew what is old!*
> *Make known what is new! From a cello the bow*
> *Draws its hauntingest tone, confiding, profound;*
> *And immured in the bone the marrow responds*
> *To the endless, exploring inventions of sound.*

William Plomer, from *Celebrations*

50. SPOOF SUFFOLK FIND

"I have no doubt that Mrs Portway will send her motor-car to fetch you
from the station. Her chauffeur, Barker by the way, is a splendid local
character, a fine specimen of East Anglian manhood, who has proved
invaluable to us, both by his knowledge of the locality and by the loan of
his considerable muscle power, which, in view of the difficulty of engaging satisfactory labour, has been very welcome . . ."

Mrs Portway's Delage had, in fact, met Gerald – a plum-coloured
motor-car with Barker in a plum-coloured uniform matching his com-
plexion. Gerald, more accustomed to such luxuries than Dr Stokesay, was
in the habit of making up for his father's taciturnity by a few polite
observations to the chauffeur. Such replies as he received from Barker,
however, were neither intelligible nor encouraging. He gave himself up to
watching as much of the countryside as could be seen through the August

dust. Rolling country, oak-wooded here and there among the buff-coloured corn, gave way to flat, marshy heath. Through the dust-choked air Gerald began to sense salt-freshened currents in the slight east wind that cut the morning's heat. Wilting loosestrife, its purple bruised, giant yarrows, their lace dried and buckled, were interspersed increasingly along the roadside by clumsy-headed bullrushes and bushes of feathery tamarisk, their growth twisted westwards by the strong sea gales. It was almost twenty miles from the station to Melpham house, but they had hardly travelled an hour before the motor-car turned into a drive lined by St John's wort and variegated hollies.

"There'll be no one at the house but the mistress," Barker remarked. "We turned up something to the west of Long Mile Meadow this morning. It seems that'd be a bishop's grave that they put out in the marshes in those times. Young Rammage came on the stone coffin digging there with young Mr Stokesay. But that's pretty deep laid. That'll take more than they've got down there to raise. The master's quite taken on with it though, says he must have it up. And Dr Stokesay, he says the same.' He was still talking as Gerald caught sight of his hostess on the steps of the square red-brick house; his tongue once loosed, it seemed that Barker could be both loquacious and intelligible.

Angus Wilson, *Anglo-Saxon Attitudes*

51. THE ORWELL

Sweet stream! on whose banks in my childhood residing,
Untutor'd by life in the lessons of care;
In the heart-cheering whispers of hope still confiding,
Futurity's prospects seem'd smiling and fair.

Dear river! how gaily the sun-beams are glancing
On thy murmuring waves, as they roll to the main!
While my tempest-tost bark, on life's ocean advancing,
Despairs of e'er finding a harbour again.

Fair Orwell! *those banks which thy billows are laving,*
Full oft have I thoughtlessly saunter'd along;
Or beneath those tall trees, which the fresh breeze is waving,
Have listen'd with rapture to nature's wild song.

But say, can thy groves, though with harmony ringing,
Recall the emotions of youthful delight?
Or can thy gay banks, where the flowerets are springing,
Revive the impressions they once could excite?

Ah no! those bright visions for ever are vanish'd,
Thy fairy dominion, sweet fancy, is o'er;
The soft-soothing whispers of hope too are banished,
The "Song of the Syren" enchants me no more.

Adieu, lovely Orwell! *for ages still flowing!*
On thy banks may the graces, and virtues combine:
Long, long may thy beauties, fresh raptures bestowing,
Diffuse the sweet pleasure they've yielded to mine.

When this head is reclined on its last clay-cold pillow
My memory forgotten, my name passed away;
May a Minstrel, more bless'd, snatch my harp from the willow,
And devote to thee, Orwell! *a worthier lay.*

Bernard Barton, *To The River Orwell*

52. SUFFOLK REVISITED

After his wife's death in 1813, Crabbe paid a last visit in early summer to Parham and Glemham: the following lines were found afterwards in his pocketbook.

Yes, I behold again the place,
The seat of joy, the source of pain;
It brings in view the form and face
That I must never see again

The night bird's song that sweetly floats
On this soft gloom – this balmy air,
Brings to the mind her sweeter notes
That I again must never hear.

Lo! yonder shines the window's light,
My guide, my token, heretofore;
And now again it shines as bright,
When those dear eyes can shine no more.

Then hurry from this place away!
It gives not now the bliss it gave;
For death has made its charm his prey,
And joy is buried in her grave.

George Crabbe

V. PLACES IN SUFFOLK

The passages following again take the reader about Suffolk, with emphasis on the features of the villages and towns which have struck past travellers. There is a marked contrast between the settlements of East Suffolk and the rest of the county.

1. THE SUFFOLK MARKET TOWN

Some in fact fall below the usually accepted threshold of town facilities. This condition may be chronic, as in much of East Suffolk.

Department of the Environment, *Strategic Choice for East Anglia*

2. THE VILLAGE

'Tis night   the weary world is still
Forgotten and alone;
I muse, upon the wooded hill,
Beneath the summer moon,
That seems as though she smiled more bright,
While listening to the bird of night!

Beside me sweeps the spreading glade;
Around me spring the flowers;
And far below, amid the shade
Of happy green wood bowers,
All bright beneath the spangled skies,
My loved and lovely village lies.

There many a high aspiring dome
And lowly cot is seen;
There many a glad and peaceful home,
Where pride nor care has been –
Where hearts are undisturbed by strife,
Unruffled on the sea of life.

And yet, perchance, of all who now
Rest there, enchained by sleep,

Some wretch may wake with throbbing brow,
And eyes unclosed, to weep:
Whose heart within its blighted core,
May feel the glow of hope no more!

Oh! in a spot so fair as this,
Which Nature's heavenly hand
Has painted for her bower of bliss,
Her Eden of the land;
In this fair spot life's stream should glide,
One sweet, unchanged, unbroken tide.

Dear, peaceful village! though from thee
My thoughts are wont to roam
To distant scenes o'er earth and sea,
Thou only art my home;
In thee alone my treasure lies –
My all of joy beneath the skies!

Here, here alone I feel the spell,
All earthly spells above;
Oh! here my friends, my children dwell,
Here smiles my own true love!
Vain world! I would not change this spot
For all thou hast and I have not.

Now sleep, the beauteous landscape fades
Beneath the waning moon;
And I forsake these lovely glades
To seek my home alone;
Still, still the scene shows fair and bright –
Thou Village of my heart! Good night!

James Bird, from the *Suffolk Garland*

3. DUNWICH

a) Edric of Laxfield held Dunwich in King Edward's time as a manor –
and now Robert Malet holds it. – Then 2 carrucates of land, now 1. The
sea carried away the other. And always 1 plough-team in demesne. Then
12 bordars, now 2.

Entry in Domesday Book

b) The toune of Dunwich, a coaste toune, neare the midle of the sheire, is scituate upon a cliffe fortie foot hie, or there about; bounded on the Easte with the Otian Sea; on the Weaste with the toune of Westleton, and is girte on the Weaste and South, neare to the bodie of the toune, with an auntient bancke, whereof parte is now builte with the wall of the Graieffriers; the North and Southe ends are environ'd with diverse marishes, shredds, and divided with fleetes, crickes, and diches; the auntient haven there was somtime at the North end of the toune, where standeth nou the Keie, which haven was utterlie choaked upp, with a North-Easte winde, the foretene daie of Januarie, Anno I Edward, III. notwithstanding if it were recovered woulde not onlie preserve the toune from danger of the sea; but bie helpe of a sluce weastwarde, woulde soe maintaine the same as might likelse bringe the same toune neare to her former estate and condition . . . Touchinge the state of the toune in times paste, it appeareth as well by their charter, as otherwise, that it hath benn one of the antienst tounes in this Yland; that there hath been a *Bishoppes Sea*, also a Minte, and a market everie daie in the week. And hath also (for their sondrie faiethfull and espetial servises, as makinge out at some one time eleven strong and well furnished shyppes, for the defence of the realme at their owne costes and charges, by the space of thirteen weakes, and more, with loss of 500 men, and 1000 £ in gooddes, etc from time to time stodd in high favour with the Kinges of this land, of whom they have received most large and liberall graunts of priviledges, liberties, customes etc. besides sundrie letters, from sutch Kinges, written to the burgesses there, for the preservation of their liberties, priviledges and customes of anchorage, mesurage, preferments of merchandiz, wreckes, groundage, arrestes and distresses partayning to the same etc., bie meane whereof they have benn from time to time, nurses, fosterers, and maintainers, for easie and reasonable toules and customes unto the people, and men of Bliborough, Walberswick and Southwold: the lorde of which Bliborough hath now in farm, the Ferie at the New-Haven for the rent but of twenty shillings a yeare to the bailiffes, burgesses and communal, of Dunwich aforesaid.

Radulph Agas, *The Report of Dunwich* (1589)

c) (During the reign of James I) a constitution was there made, that every *crayer* trading to Westmona, North-Seas, Iceland and Farra, should pay to the town's use annually eight shillings, on the first of September.

Thomas Gardiner, *History of Dunwich*

d) A vision of grey-roofed houses and a long winding street and the sound of many bells came over me at that word as I nodded "Yes" to him, my mouth full of salt pork and rye-bread; and then I lifted my pot and we made the clattering mugs kiss and I drank, and the fire of the good Kentish mead ran through my veins and deepened my dream of things past, present, and to come, as I said: "Now hearken a tale since ye will have it so. For last autumn I was in Suffolk at the good town of Dunwich, and thither came the keels from Iceland, and on them were some men of Iceland, and many a tale they had on their tongues; and with these men I foregathered, for I am in sooth a gatherer of tales, and this that is now at my tongue's end is one of them."

So such a tale I told them, long familiar to me; but as I told it the words seemed to quicken and grow, so that I knew not the sound of my own voice, and they ran almost into rhyme and measure as I told it; and when I had done there was silence awhile, till one man spake, but not loudly:

"Yea, in that land was the summer short and the winter long; but men lived both summer and winter; and if the trees grew ill and the corn throve not, yet did the plant called man thrive and do well. God send us such men even here."

William Morris, *A Dream of John Ball*

e) THE SITE OF DUNWICH

Where the lone cliff uprears its rugged head,
Where frowns the ruin o'er the silent dead,
Where sweeps the billow on the lonely shore,
Where once the mighty lived, but live no more;
Where proudly frowned the convent's massy wall,
Where rose the gothic tower, the stately hall,
Where bards proclaimed, and warriors shared the feast,
Where ruled the baron, and where knelt the priest, –
There stood the city in its pride – 'tis gone!
Mocked at by crumbling pile, and mouldering stone,
And shapeless masses which the reckless power
Of time hath hurled from ruined arch and tower!
O'er the lone spot, where shrines and pillared halls
Once gorgeous shone, the clammy lizard crawls;
O'er the lone spot, where yawned the guarded fosse,
Creeps the wild bramble, and the spreading moss:
Oh! time hath bowed that lordly city's brow,
In which the mighty dwelt – where dwell they now?

James Bird

f) As the ruin of this town was principally owing to the encroachments of the sea from time to time, it will not be improper to give here a more particular account of these dreadful devastations. It is observable that the coast is here destitute of rocks, and the principal part of Dunwich being built on a hill, consisting of loam and sand of a loose texture, it is no wonder that the surges of the sea, beating against the foot of the precipice, easily undermined it. – Gardner, in his historical account of Dunwich, observes that one of the two carves of land, taxed in the reign of Edward the Confessor, was found to be swallowed up by the sea, at the time of the survey made by order of William the Conqueror. The church of St. Felix, and the cell of monks, were lost very early. In the first year of Edward the Third the old port was rendered entirely useless, and before the 23rd year of that king's reign, great part of the town, with upwards of 400 houses, which paid rent to the fee-farm, with certain shops and windmills, were devoured by the sea. After this the church of St. Leonard was overthrown; and in the 14th century the churches of St. Martin and St. Nicholas were also destroyed by the waves. In 1540 the church of St. John Baptist was taken down, and in the same centuries, the chapels of St. Anthony, St. Francis and St. Catharine were overthrown, with the South Gate and Gilden Gate, and not one quarter of the town left standing. In the reign of Charles the First, the foundation of the Temple Buildings yielded to the irresistible force of the undermining surges, and in 1677 the sea reached the market place. In 1680 all the buildings north of Maison Dieu lane were demolished, and in 1702 the sea extended its dominion to St. Peter's Church, on which it was divested of the lead, timber, bells and other materials, the walls only remaining, which tumbled over the cliff as the water undermined them; and the town hall suffered the same fate. In 1715 the jail was undermined, and in 1729 the farthest bounds of St. Peter's churchyard fell into the sea.

In December 1740, the wind blowing very hard from the north-east, and continuing for several days, occasioned terrible devastations; for a great part of the cliffs were washed away, with the remains of St. Nicholas's churchyard, as also the great road which formerly led into the town. – King's-holm, otherwise called Leonard's-marsh, which was then worth 100 £ a year, was laid under water, and has ever since been so covered with shingles and sand, that it is now worth little. Besides, Cock and Hen hills, which the preceding summer were upwards of 40 feet high, had their heads levelled with their bases; and the foundation of St. Francis's chapel was discovered. Several skeletons appeared on the Ouse, some lying in pretty good order, and others scattered about by the waves. At the same time, near the chapel, were found the pipes of an ancient aqueduct, some of which were of lead, and others of a grey earth, like that of some urns.

G. A. Cooke, *Topographical and Statistical Description of Suffolk*

g) "It's a sweet little queer, quaint, surviving corner of a wonderful place, one is assured, long since devoured by the cold North Sea, – primitive and rough, but with a very delicate and delightful charm . . . I don't know the East Coast to speak of at all – and I can imagine no more winsome introduction to it."

Henry James, Letter quoted by H. Montgomery Hyde, in *Henry James at Home.*

h) *Swinburne stayed in Dunwich prior to composition of the following.*

BY THE NORTH SEA

A land that is lonelier than ruin;
A sea that is stranger than death:
Far fields that a rose never blew in,
Wan waste where the winds lack breath;
Waste endless and boundless and flowerless
But of marsh-blossoms fruitless as free:
Where earth lies exhausted, as powerless
To strive with the sea.

Far flickers the flight of the swallows,
Far flutters the weft of the grass
Spun dense over desolate hollows
More pale than the clouds as they pass:
Thick woven as the weft of a witch is
Round the heart of a thrall that hath sinned,
Whose youth and the wrecks of its riches
Are waifs on the wind.

The pastures are herdless and sheepless,
No pasture or shelter for herds:
The wind is relentless and sleepless
And restless and songless the birds;
Their cries from afar fall breathless,
Their wings are as lightnings that flee;
For the land has two lords that are deathless:
Death's self, and the sea.

These twain, as a king with his fellow,
Hold converse of desolate speech:
And the waters are haggard and yellow
And crass with the scurf of the beach:

And his garments are gray as the hoary
Wan sky where the day lies dim;
And his power is to her, and his glory,
As hers unto him.

Algernon Charles Swinburne, from *By The North Sea*

4. SOUTHWOLD

Southwold, on the sea-coast, about two miles from Reydon, was probably named from the wood near it, as the western confines still retain the appellation of Wood's End Creek. It is pleasantly situated on a hill over-looking the German ocean, but nearly encompassed by the river Blyth, over which a bridge leads into the town. It was originally a small place, consisting only of a few fishermen's huts; but in proportion as they were successful, they built houses, and at length became rivals to Dunwich and other neighbouring towns. Alfric, bishop of the East Angles, gave this lordship, among many other donations, to the abbey of Bury St. Edmunds, by which it was held as one manor, for victualling the monks. Under Henry IV Southwold was exempted from the payment of any customs or tolls, for their small boats passing in or out of the river or port of Dunwich. Henry VII, in consideration of the industry and good ser-vices of the men of Southwold, made the town a free burgh, or corpora-tion, to be governed by two bailiffs, a recorder, and other inferior officers. This town had several benefactions from that king and his son Henry VIII, which enabled the merchants to fit out upwards of fifty vessels, and these they employed abroad in the cod fishery, while the industry of those employed on the coast, in catching herrings and other fish, was also very conducive to the improvement of the town; but when Henry VIII shook off the pope's supremacy, the fishery began to decline, though the inhab-itants still carried it on, and at the same time engaged in the trade of corn, malt, timber, coals, butter and cheese.

On the 25th of April, 1659, there happened a dreadful fire at Southwold, which, in the space of four hours, consumed the town-hall and market-house, prison, granaries, warehouses and 238 dwelling houses, besides the fish-houses, tackle-houses and other out-houses; and the greatest part of the moveable goods, nets, and tackle of the inhabitants, with all their corn, fish, coals, and other commodities; the loss of which amounted to upwards of 40,000 £, an immense sum at that time, and ruined above 300 families. This disaster obliged many to seek for habita-tions in other places, insomuch that the town, which was in a flourishing condition previous to this dreadful calamity, never recovered its former splendour. All the court-baron rolls were destroyed, by which means the copyholders of the parish became freeholders.

However, the trade of Southwold was considerably promoted, in consequence of an act of parliament, passed for repairing and improving the harbour, which being subject to be choked up, a pier was erected on the north side of the port in 1749, and another on the south in 1752. When the free British fishery began to be established in 1740, the Pelham and Carteret busses arrived in this harbour from Shetland, and in 1751 buildings and conveniences began to be erected for the making and tanning of nets, and depositing stores; two docks were also made, and many other improvements, so that, in 1753, no less than thirty-eight busses sailed from this port. The other trade of this place consists in the home fishery, which employs several small boats; and here they make and refine salt, prepare and export red herrings, red sprats, malt and corn; and import coals, cinders and the like. The inhabitants likewise carry on a coasting trade in wool, corn, timber and lime.

Thomas Cromwell, *Excursions in the County of Suffolk*

Fishing was obviously of great importance to the coastal settlements of Suffolk, and the following extract, from the Ipswich Journal, is typical of several.

5. LOWESTOFT

a) Whereas it has been represented and repeated, by some ill-designing people, that the Boats do not go to sea from Lowestoft to catch mackarels as usual, on account of the war with France: This is to give notice to all buyers and others, that we have now at sea thirteen boats, employed in catching mackarels, and that during the season, all Pedlars and others may be duly supplied with the said Fish at Lowestoft as in former years.

Notice in the Ipswich Journal 5 June 1744

b) His eyes were all over the place. There was such a lot to see in this harbour. He looked at the swing bridge, closed now, with carts and motor cars and people going across it. He looked along the quay to the Custom House with the big crest over the doorway, and beyond it the tall masts of the fishing vessels. He looked up the inner harbour towards the dry dock, where a steam trawler was being repaired and there was a great noise of men chipping rust and riveting ... The Wind freshened a little, and *Swallow* felt it. She was moving very fast. They had just time to read the name painted in big white letters across the stern of the schooner,

"VIPER: BRISTOL", and then they were slipping away towards the bridge and hoping that the puff of wind would last them through it.

"What a funny name for a boat," said Roger.

They had a fine sail round the outer harbour, looking into one basin after another. They saw the Government fishery vessel, with the reindeer horns from Lapland fastened up on the bridge. They watched one of the fishing ketches sail out between the pier heads. "That's where we'll be going tomorrow," said Nancy. Then John gave Nancy the tiller, and she sailed the *Swallow* into Hamilton Dock, where they saw the steam trawlers. By that time Susan and Peggy were thinking they ought to be putting a kettle on to boil, so they sailed back, though they had to use oars in getting through under the swing bridge. They put the cooks aboard, and then John, Nancy, Titty, and Roger went off for a last half-hour of sailing.

They tacked away up the inner harbour, past the dry dock and the vessels being repaired, past the grey dredgers at work getting up the mud from the bottom. They did not go very far before turning back.

Arthur Ransome, *Peter Duck*

6. ALDEBURGH

a) Aldeburgh is a town pleasantly situate in the Valley of Slaughden, extending itself near a mile from North to South; but it is not very broad from East to West. Its breadth has formerly been more than it is now, the unkind ocean has in this age swallowed up one whole street. At present there are two streets very near a mile in length. The town is meanly built, but very clean. The ocean washes the East side of the town, and the River Ald runs not far from the south end thereof affording a good key at Slaughden. The chief trade of this town is fishing for herrings in the adjacent seas, in their seasons; yet it trades for coals to Newcastle, and corn is transported from hence to other parts. It is tolerably situate for strength, and has several pieces of cannon for its defence. The church stands on a hill a little west of the town, and is a very good structure. It is a town corporate, governed by two bailiffs, ten capital burgesses, and 24 inferiour officers. It enjoys divers privileges, sending two members to Parliament etc. Here is a small market weekly on Saturdays, and two fairs yearly, the one on the 3rd of September, and the other on the first Tuesday in Lent.

Thus much for Aldeburgh.

John Kirby, *The Suffolk Traveller* (1st Ed.)

b) In the summer months Aldeburgh awoke and became a place of gayness and jollity for a brief spell. The high spot of the whole year was the Regatta, when the town was filled with strangers, and all the old sleepy drinking houses did a roaring trade. The night was shattered by the brazen music of the round-a-bouts and scenic railways, and the cries of the vendors of the rock. Never will I forget that "Fair Rock" of all colours, shapes, sizes and flavours, nor the mountainous piles of golden brown "brandy snaps", crisp and sticky, all made by hand as the fascinated onlookers gaped on. The stalls where one could sup on oysters, or little plates of cockles, liberally besprinkled with vinegar and pepper, or saucers of huge rubbery whelks. Another stall, painted a brilliant red, sold fish and chips, which were advertised far afield by the savoury smell. There were dart booths where for a score of twenty-five or over one could procure a vase of wondrous glistening beauty, or a box of chocolates. Cheek by jowl with the shooting gallery was a stall where one could buy bags of confetti and small tubes of water known as "squirts". Loud feminine shrieks and squeals told of the good use to which the confetti was being put. The shout of the showman at the booth of the Fat Lady and Skeleton Man vied with the cry of the man at the boxing saloon, where one could pound and be pounded for the entrance fee of sixpence. Well do I remember the flare of naptha and rumble of the scenic railway, interwoven with the hubbub of closely-packed humanity, the creak and swish of the swinging boats, and the whizz of the chair-o-planes. The fair lasted a whole week, a whirling, riotous week of yacht races, rowing races, swimming races for dogs, climbing the greasy pole, the Procession, and the Fancy Dress Parade. Everyone was infected by the spirit of Carnival. There was dancing and drinking, and love-making on the summer beach.

It seems strange that the gay spirit of a continental Mardi Gras should invade that remote townlet, which stands, desolate and lonely, on the very brink of the cold North Sea, where the nights are still unconsciously fraught with the thousand-year-old dread of the long black Dragon Boats.

George Carter, *Looming Lights*

c) Two hundred years ago, Aldborough was a place of considerable importance, but repeated incroachments of the sea reduced it to the rank of a small and insignificant fishing town. During the last century, the ocean made great ravages, and in the recollection of persons yet living, destroyed many houses, together with the Market place and the Cross. It does not, however, appear from any ancient records, that Aldborough ever contained public buildings of extent or consequence; nor has there at any time been discovered vestiges, which could convey an idea of ancient splendour and magnificence. From an accurate plan of the borough, which was taken in 1559, and which is still extant, it appears to have been, at that time, a place of considerable magnitude, and that the greater portion of the town was built to the eastward of the present inn, the White Lion, which then formed a part of the western side of the market place. From the same document it also appears that the church was then more than ten times its present distance from the shore; and also that there were DENES of some extent, similar to those at Yarmouth between the town and the sea, which have long been swallowed up and lost. After very high tides, the remains of wells have been frequently discovered below high water mark; and about eleven or twelve years ago, seventeen were distinctly visible.

Seated upon a hill, composed of loam and sand of a loose texture, it is not surprising that its buildings should have successively yielded to the impetuosity of the billows, constantly breaking against and easily undermining the foot of the precipice, and thus become an easy prey to their repeated encroachments . . .

Nothing, indeed, could be more gloomy and disheartening than was formerly the approach to this town. On every side a wild, desolate and barren country disclosed one uniform and cheerless aspect; whilst the deep-rutted, or heavy, sandy roads presented difficulties to the weary and jaded traveller, which frequently occasioned him no small apprehension even for his personal safety.

James Ford, *Aldborough Described: Full Description of that Fashionable and much Frequented Watering Place*

d) Aldeburgh in the 17th century, both in size and appearance, must have differed considerably from the present town, and the same remark applies to many of the leading features of its immediate neighbourhood. The town itself, by several streets, was wider than it is now, and contained many more houses and cottages, but some things remain now as they were then, eg we find a mention of the "Lion" in 1647, the landlord of which, Richard Groby, was then paid "14s 8d by Mr. Bailiff's order, for diet and wine, when Capt. Wenhall was ashore, hurt, that was convoy for the Iceland barks." If we may judge from a sale made in 1683, property, at that period, was not very valuable, for we find a record that one pound was paid by Mr. J. Coggeshall to the Corporation for an "ould cottage" purchased of them. The Haven, towards Thorpe, was so far navigable that ships of considerable burthen used to lie there during the winter and other months . . . At either end of the town of Aldeburgh were large marshes, or, as expressed in another place, heaths, and here in 1626 the Dunkirkers landed. We are not told what damage they committed, but a charge is recorded of 1s 4d for beer for the men (that is townspeople) for "carrying to and again"; probably this refers to some means of resistance employed. It is, however, conclusive evidence that the whole of the inhabitants, even at that period, were not teetotalers.

"The humble certificate of the Dep.-Lieut. of the County of Suff. touching the Towne of Aldeburgh, in the county, 1626.

"1 Certifye that the said towne is situated upon the mayne sea, verie open to invasion, within 12 hours' sail of Dunkirk, and that the passage from thence is without danger of sands, and it is greatlee to be feared that the Dunkirk will assail the said towne.

"2 Item, that the shore against the said town is so deepe, that, by reason of the marshes at both ends of the towne, there may be landed by boats and shippes 10,000 men in an hour's space, which may fire the towne and take the village through before the country can come to aid them.

"3 Item, there is no bulwark for fortification against the said towne, to defend it from the enemy, but only viii pieces of small iron ordinance, which are all honeycombe, and not fitt for service. And the said towne, being one of the greatest townes in that part of the country for landing by sea and maintaining of mariners and seafaring men, and also being situate near the common road and passage for shippes to Newcastle and other Ports of the North, hath as great need for fortifications as any towne in the said county, both for defence of themselves and their friends.

"4 Item, that a fleet of shippes may ride within muskett shott of the said towne, and the sea shore being all beach and shingle, upon which the said pieces of ordinance stand, is open to the enemy, without any shelter or defence, so that if a shot come from the enemy and beats upon the shingle, the said shott will hazard to kill the gunner and all those about him, or at least drive them from the ordinance.

"5 Item, in the tyme of service and trade by sea, the greatest parte of the inhabitants of the said towne, being seafaring men, are gone to sea, and leave the town destitute of any great number of serviceable men, not able to resist any great forces, unless there be some fortification made.

"6 Item, the said towne hath already been at great charge about the mountinge of the said pieces of ordinance, although they be of little use, and now not able to fortify the same towne, it being of late much impoverished and many other ways changed."

N. F. Hele, *Notes and Jottings about Aldeburgh*

e) . . . It is reckoned by the physicians to be one of the most healthy places along the coast, and as remarkable for longevity, being subject to cooling and refreshing breezes from the sea, on which account a great deal of company resort to the town in summer for the benefit of their health and sea bathing, to which the pleasantness of the spot invites; and is growing into much repute. The shore is also much admired for its evenness and regular declivity for the bathing machines, which are upon a remarkably safe and commodious construction. The hills at the back of the town are likewise much esteemed for the pleasant walks, and for the fine and beautiful prospects of the surrounding country for many miles.

G. A. Cooke, *Topographical and Statistical Description of Suffolk*

f) That miserable dull sea village, the sound of whose waves never went out of George's ears.

Virginia Woolf, *George Crabbe, From Collected Essays.*

g) The situation of the place is curious. A slight rise of the ground – I'll call it a hill, though the word is too emphatic – projects from the fenlands of Suffolk towards the North Sea. On this hill stands the church, a spacious Gothic building with very broad aisles, so that it has inside rather the effect of a hall. At the foot of the hill lies the town – a couple of long streets against which the sea is making an implacable advance. There used to be as many as five streets – three of them have disappeared beneath the shallow but violent waters, the house where Crabbe was born is gone, the street that has been named after him is menaced, the Elizabethan moot hall, which used to be in the centre of the place, now stands on a desolate beach. During the past twelve months the attack has been frightening. I can remember a little shelter erected for visitors on the shingle. Last autumn it was at the edge of a cliff, so that fishermen at the high tide actually sat in it to fish. This spring it has vanished, and the waters actually broke into the High Street – huge glassy waves coming in regularly and quietly, and each exploding when it hit the shore with the sound of a gun. This sort of attack went on a hundred and fifty years ago, when Crabbe was alive, but the zone of operation lay further out. Today, only the hill is safe. Only at the church, where he preached, and where his parents lie buried, is there security and peace.

North and south of the hill lie marshes. The marshland to the north requires no comment, but that to the south is peculiar, and I had it in mind when I called the situation of Aldeburgh 'curious'. It is intersected by the river Alde which flows due east – but when it is within fifty yards of the sea it turns due south, and does not reach the sea for twelve miles, being divided from it by a narrow ridge of shingle. Here again the waves are attacking, and are trying to break through the barrier that keeps them from the river. If they succeed – and they have had some success –

Aldeburgh will be menaced on its flank and the valuable town grazing lands will disappear into the slime of the estuary.

It is with this estuary of the Alde that we are mainly concerned today. It is here, and not on the open sea or the sea front, that the action of the poem of 'Peter Grimes' takes place. There used to be a little port on the estuary, Slaughden Quay. It was important in Crabbe's day, and was well defined even in my own earlier visits to the district. It is now battered and derelict and the sea may wash across into it at the next great storm. Here Crabbe worked as a boy, rolling casks of butter about, and much he hated it. Hence Peter Grimes set out to fish. The prospect from Slaughden, despite desolation and menace, is romantic. At low tide the great mud flats stretch. At high tide the whole area is a swirl of many-coloured waters. At all times there are birds and low woodlands on the farther bank, and, to the north, Aldeburgh sheltering among a few trees, and still just managing to dominate her fate.

E. M. Forster, 'George Crabbe and Peter Grimes', from *Two Cheers for Democracy*

7. ORFORD

a) Oreford, now commonly called Orford, is situate on the North-west side of the River Ore, and so took its name of Oreford. Most of our historians say it is situate on the River Ore, where it empties itself into the River Ald, which is notoriously false; for the conjunction of those rivers are about a mile South-east of Glemham Parva Church, and therefore could never be where Orford now is. It was anciently a town of good account, having a strong castle for its defence, which formerly belonged to the Valoines, afterwards to the de Uffords, and now to the Hon. Pryce D'Evereux Esq; son and heir apparent to the Right Hon. the Lord Viscount Hereford. Other towns on this coast complain of the incursions of the sea upon them; but this town has more reason to complain of the sea's unkindness, which withdrawing itself seems to envy it the advantage of an harbour.

John Kirby, *The Suffolk Traveller* (1st Ed.)

8. SHINGLE STREET

There were occasional glorious days when he was able to borrow a boat and take the whole family out sailing. There were also long days of walking in the country when he taught his children to stride with their short legs along the Suffolk lanes and footpaths that he knew so well.

The children spent their summer holidays in a farmhouse belonging to their nurse's uncle. It was near Butley, about thirty miles south of Lowestoft. Here the walks were across the marshes, with the wind blowing from the sea. As they went on their way, the tall reeds and rushes moved with them, leaning over with a swishing sound, while high overhead the curlews and redshanks called to each other. Beyond the marshes, the farthest walks led to Shingle Street, a small row of cottages on a pebbly beach, where there was nothing in sight except a vast expanse of sea and sky. Shingle Street has altered very little since those Augusts at the end of the First World War. The stony shelf of pebbles stretches for mile after mile into the distance. On a still day, the light can have the delicate outlines of a Japanese picture. On a stormy day, even in summer, the grey sea batters itself against the shelf, dragging the shingle down with a scrunching, grating, slithering sound. To anyone who lives on the Suffolk coast, this sound means home.

Imogen Holst, *Britten*

9. BAWDSEY

At this time the shores of Norfolk and Suffolk were most conspicuous for contraband trade. Severe and deadly were the continual actions between the preventive-service men and the smugglers; lives were continually lost on both sides; and dreadful animosities sprang up between the parties upon the sea-shore.

Will Laud and his associates had great luck; and Captain Bargood found him as bold and profitable a fellow as he could wish. Many were the hairbreadth escapes, however, which he, in conjunction with his crew, experienced. Laud was a tool in the hands of his mate, though he himself was not aware of it; for whilst that fellow had his own way, he always managed to get it through the medium of the captain's permission. He would, in his bluff way, suggest, with all becoming sub-ordination, such and such a scheme, and generally succeeded in the enterprise.

They had observed for a long time a scout upon the beach under Bawdsey Cliffs, and knew that he was one of the Irish cruisers, who had been transplanted to watch their craft: Laud proposed to nab him when he could. He had been ashore one day to meet his employer, and had met this merry-hearted Irishman at the Sun Inn, in the street of that long, sandy village of Bawdsey. Pat was a loquacious, whisky-loving, light-hearted fellow, who, without fear, and with ready wit, made himself agreeable to everybody. He frequented the various inns along the border, and was generally liked for his dash of gallantry, his love of drinking, and his generous spirit; he was a brave fellow, too, and watchful for his honour. He had seen along the beach a man roaming about, and had concealed himself, not far from a fisherman's cottage, on purpose to watch him; but all he could make out was, that the man went to the back of the cottage, and there he lost him. Pat went to the fisherman's cot, found the man and his wife at their meals, searched about the premises, but could spy nothing. Pat had seen this thing several times, and was fully convinced that the man he saw was a smuggler.

In Bawdsey Cliff the smugglers had a cave of no small dimensions. It had formerly been a hollow ravine in the earth, formed by the whirling of a stream of water, which had passed quickly through a gravelly bed, and met with opposition in this mass of clay. It had made for itself a large crater, and then had issued again at the same place, and ran through a sand-gall and gravelly passage down to the sea. This was discovered by a tenant of the Earl of Dysart, who, in sinking a well near his shepherd's cottage, suddenly struck into the opening of this cave. As the springs were low at this season, the cave was almost empty of water, and formed a most curious appearance. It was even then called the Robbers' Cave, and curiosity was greatly excited in the country to visit it. It was so smoothly and regularly formed by the eddies of the whirlpool, that the nicest art could not have made it so uniform. The proprietor sank his well some feet lower, until he came to a good stream; but in making the well, he formed an archway into this curious place, and left it so for the gratification of public curiosity. Time swept on, and the cave became less frequented, and at last forgotten.

A few years, however, previously to this narrative, some smugglers had been disappointed of their run, and had thrown their tubs down the well, with the consent of their agent the fisherman, probably a descendant of the old shepherd's, who dwelt in the cottage. This led to the re-discovery and improvement of this famous depot of arms, ammunition, stock-in-trade, and place of retreat, which was then occupied by Will Laud and his associates, and to which very spot John Luff was at that time bound.

These men had contrived to make the cave as comfortable a berth as a subterraneous place could be. They had ingeniously tapped the land stream below the cave, and laid it perfectly dry, and with much labour and ingenuity had contrived to perforate the clay into the very chimney of the cottage; so that a current of air passed through the archway directly up the chimney, and carried away the smoke, without the least suspicion being awakened. This place was furnished with tables, mats, stools, and every requisite for a place of retreat and rendezvous. The descent was by the bucket well-rope, which a sailor well knew how to handle; whilst the bucket itself served to convey provisions or goods of any kind.

Rev Richard Cobbold, *The History of Margaret Catchpole*

10. FELIXSTOWE

or

The Last of Her Order

With one consuming roar along the shingle
The long wave claws and rakes the pebbles down
To where its backwash and the next wave mingle,
A mounting arch of water weedy-brown
Against the tide of off-shore breezes blow.
Oh wind and water, this is Felixstowe.

In winter when the sea winds chill and shriller
Than those of summer, all their cold unload
Full on the gimcrack attic of the villa
Where I am lodging off the Orwell Road,
I put my final shilling in the meter
And only make my loneliness completer.

In eighteen ninety-four when we were founded,
Counting our Reverend Mother we were six,
How full of hope we were and prayer-surrounded
"The Little Sisters of the Hanging Pyx".
We built our orphanage. We ran our school.
Now only I am left to keep the rule.

Here in the gardens of the Spa Pavilion
Warm in the whisper of a summer sea,
The cushioned scabious, a deep vermilion,
With white pins stuck in it, looks up at me
A sun-lit kingdom touched by butterflies
And so my memory of winter dies.

Across the grass the poplar shades grow longer
And louder clang the waves along the coast.
The band packs up. The evening breeze is stronger
And all the world goes home to tea and toast.
I hurry past a cakeshop's tempting scones
Bound for the red brick twilight of St. John's.

"Thou knowest my down sitting and mine uprising"
Here where the white light burns with steady glow
Safe from the vain world's silly sympathising,
Safe with the Love that I was born to know,
Safe from the surging of the lonely sea
My heart finds rest, my heart finds rest in Thee.

John Betjeman, *Collected Poems*

11. WOODBRIDGE

a) Woodbridge has nothing remarkable, but that it is a considerable market for butter and corn to be exported to London; for now begins that part which is ordinarily called High-Suffolk . . .

Daniel Defoe, *A Tour Through the Whole Island of Great Britain*

b) The 5th of July, 1633, being a Friday, I began a journey from Chatham by sea into Suffolk in the little Henrietta pinnace commanded by Captain Cook, one of the Master Attendants of his Majesty's Navy, accompanied with young Mr. Henry Palmer, Mr. Isackson, son Yardley, cousin Joseph, my sons Peter and Christopher, man Charles Bowles, and George Parker. We set sail from Gillingham in the morning, having a fair gale at south-west. We anchored against Harwich, between two and three of the clock, afternoon, and from thence shipped ourselves and company in boats for Ipswich, arriving there afore 6 in the evening, and lodged at the Angel Inn, which was then kept by my cousin Barwick. On Saturday morning we were horsed to Woodbridge on hackneys, whither we came about 11 of the clock and were lodged at the Crown. After dinner we went to visit Mrs. Cole and her daughters, with whom we had large discourse about the match of her daughter with my son Peter, and found our propositions entertained, I having great liking to the maid. Sunday, we and our train dined and supped at Mrs. Cole's. Monday, we invited mother and daughters and Mr. Fleming to dine with us at our inn, whither came to us divers of our friends to whom we gave the best entertainment the place could afford. In the afternoon we had private conferences together, and concluded the match and contracted the parties with free consent on both sides; we supped this night at Mrs. Cole's. Tuesday forenoon, having despatched all our business, we took our journey by horse to Landguard Point accompanied by Mistress Cole, her daughters, and other their friends and neighbours, whom we entertained a while on board our pinnace, and there resolved the day of marriage; thence we accompanied them on shore, saw them horsed, and so took leave. My son and some other of the company accompanied them to Woodbridge, being overtaken with a mighty storm of rain, thunder and lightning all the way.

Phineas Pett, *Autobiography*

c) It had been arranged by Jewsuf, and mournfully agreed to by Mrs. Thirkettle, that she should not confess her theft to her husband until her son had had time to leave the country. The three days that elapsed were days of purgatory to the poor woman.

Thursday came, the Stonebridge market day. Bethuel and Dinah drove off together in the rickety old gig with five tuneful little pigs netted in at the back; but they no more heeded the familiar cries than a London lady is disturbed by the roar and rattle of the streets when she drives through them in her brougham. It was May, and the clay ridge was beautiful. The hedges were white with hawthorn and fragrant with the almond scent of the blossom; the meadows were gay with buttercups and rich with tender spring grass, and the deep ditches were clothed by vividly pink campion. The distances were bathed in pale blue mist; the 'dag' which had lain along the valleys had floated away, and every tender bough and blade of grass sparkled with drops of water. The old guelder-rose bush in the moated garden was covered with pale green May-balls that were hourly growing white, and the sunny freshness of the spring air and the song of the 'mavishes' and the nightingales in the quickset hedge floated in at the kitchen window where Ursula Thirkettle stood, trying to pare the potatoes that lay in a little brown heap before her, shining with washing and scrubbing. The heavy salt tears crept down her careworn face. She had been all her life scrupulously, delicately honest, and now it was in dishonesty that she had sinned, so at least it seemed to her. 'That wer wholly the same with Moses, that wer,' she thought. 'He wer the meekest man that walked the earth, so the Old Book say. And yet he make a sad mistake once through lack of meekness, and we know he never com to the Promised Land.'

Earlier than was his wont the farmer came home. Ursula saw at once, in his face, that something had happened. He went straight upstairs to the bedroom where his money was kept. Mrs. Thirkettle caught hold of Dinah's arm.

'What hev your fah-ther happened on, gal?' she cried.

'Somethin' about a rick, and Jewsuf, mother, but I dun' knaw nawthin' roightly about it.'

Dinah moved ponderously out of the room and up the creaking stairs to her room, where she took off her market-day finery and put it away in an old oak 'hutch' or chest. While she did this, slowly and methodically, a tragedy was going on downstairs. The farmer came white and speechless into the kitchen. He stood facing his wife with such a terrible look in his eyes that she fell upon her knees and hid her face in her hands. The homely kitchen where she had spent so much of her life suddenly became a torture-chamber of unknown horror. Everything seemed to have lost its familiar aspect, and to have become strange and monstrous. After a while words came to Bethuel. He lifted up his right arm and he cursed the wretched woman; cursed her with a wonderful Biblical rhythm – in her going out and her coming in; in her waking and in her sleeping; in her lying down and in her uprising; in her life and in her death, and at the Judgement Day. The blood ran backwards in her veins as she listened. She had hoped he would have struck her: any blows, any death-stroke would have been better than this. He bade her begone; she was no wife of his. Then silence fell again upon him, and Mrs. Thirkettle crept up the stairs.

Presently Dinah came to her. 'That fare a roight bad job, mother, that do,' she said, staring fixedly at Mrs. Thirkettle with her dull round eyes. 'You hed best goo to uncle's, at Stonebridge. He say he can't put up with the mawther he hev, not noohow. She'll hev to goo, I suppose, and you can stop along of him.'

There was a stock of common-sense underlying Dinah's stolidity that the family had already found helpful in emergencies. Mrs. Thirkettle let her daughter set her like a child in a chair, while she collected for her a few articles and made them into a bundle. Then Dinah dressed her mother in her Sunday bonnet and shawl. By this time the farm lad had finished milking, and Dinah bade him harness the pony in the gig and drive the missus to Stonebridge. When she had seen the poor dazed woman into the gig, she went into the kitchen to prepare the farmer's tea. Nothing that happened ever could put Dinah's mechanism out of order.

Stonebridge is a little old-fashioned town on the steep slope of a hill above a tidal river. The red roofs cluster thickly and irregularly to the left of the market-place and of the stately church, with its quiet graveyard and honey-scented lime avenue down to the river, that is sometimes a broad river of lucent silver water winding between the low hills, and sometimes a waste of brown mud and weed that takes beautiful ripe shades of russet and purple when the sun shines. The town is a little antiquated place, full of vague traditions of past glories. There is a market, chiefly of pigs, every Thursday, which still keeps the town alive. Markets are the one occasion upon which lonely country folk, dwelling in remote corners of a country intersected by the sea, can meet and be in touch for a moment with the outer world. Then the weekly store of groceries is bought; and then too, the women see the 'fashions' in the shops, spending hours of indecision over the purchase of a print gown, fingering the stuffs cunningly with their heads on one side and an air of suspicion pervading their persons, and finally parting with the cherished shillings with a sigh, counting out deliberately the sixpences, the threepenny bits, and the halfpence from unwieldy leather purses, with hands encased in big black thread gloves that stick out half an inch or more beyond the thick work-a-day fingers. Mrs. Thirkettle's bachelor brother was a linendraper, whose little shop fronted the market place. The small dingy kitchen and living-room where she now spent most of her time looked over the graveyard, away to the meadows and the big trees where the rooks built every spring, but it seemed to Mrs. Thirkettle as though the town hemmed her in and suffocated her. The poor woman lived on as if in a nightmare. Curses and blessings are not what they were to the world in general. But in quiet country places, and above all in simple hearts, the faith in them lives on, and to this day works their fulfilment in a way that is almost miraculous. Ursula felt as the excommunicated in the Middle Ages must have felt – banned, exiled, a leper.

Mrs. Thirkettle suffered keenly from homesickness. 'Stonebridge is rare and fine,' she would say apologetically to her brother, 'but that isn't my native.' The cry of her heart was for her 'native', for the long clay ridge, the forlorn moated farm, and the familiar kitchen that was for her the centre of the earth. Her cheeks grew hollow and her eyes as wistful as those of a dog; she was, as she said, 'kind o' poining for her native'.

Lady E. C. Gurdon, *Suffolk Tales – Memories and Fancies*

12. Saxmundham

We made our midday halt at Saxmundham, a quiet little market-town, pleasantly situated in the midst of a well-wooded country, one of those picturesque old-fashioned places that in a commercial age are so charmingly uncommercially unprogressive, and unspoilt by growing suburbs; looking now, doubtless, much as it did a century ago, and as in all probability it will look a century hence. A slumbrous town that wakes up into some semblance of activity one day in seven, when the market is held there, and farmers and their wives jog in from the country round to do a little business and a good deal of gossip. An uneventful existence these Saxmundhams appear to lead, but a comfortable and contented one withal, untroubled by the keen competitive spirit of the age.

The Bell Inn, with its spacious yard, seems to have changed not at all since the last coach ceased to run this way; even the legend 'Posting House' still remains plainly painted on its olden walls, but where are the 'jolly post-boys' and the ever ready post-horses? Here we had an excellent meal in a delightfully cool old-fashioned room, our fare cold roast beef and freshly gathered salad, with cheese to follow, washed down by good old English ale, clear and sparkling, a repast fit for a king; at least had I been a king then, I could not have wished for better cheer.

James John Hissey, *A Tour in a Phaeton Through the Eastern Counties*

13. Framlingham

a) One Henry Framlingham, communely caullid by office Henry Surveyar, was a stout fellow and had faire lande in and about Framelingham toune.

And after cam one Jenkin Framelingham, and purchacid a faire lord-ship and manor place about Debenham market a mile from Some in Southfolk. This maner place stondith on a praty hille and a wood aboute it a litle withoute Debenham market toune, and is caullid Crowis Haulle. For one Crow a gentilman was owner of it, or ever Jenkin Framelingham bought it. This Jenkin lyith yn Debenham church: and sins the Framelinghams hath bene lordes of the toune of Debenham. The Framelinghams of late exchaungid with the lordes of Northfolk and Wingefeld for their landes in Framelingham self, and in sum other partes very nere to it.

Ther be no mo of the Framelinghams that be men of landes there but the onely Framelingham of Debenham.

John Leland, *Itinerary*

14. BOTESDALE

Botesdale, a fine example of the single-street towns of East Anglia (Kirby calls it a long thorough-fare town) differs greatly from the compact little town of my birth. It is so long, that I am guilty of no Irishism in saying that it lies for the most part in the next parish; for, though the whole thoroughfare goes by the name of Botesdale with the gentry, or 'Buzzle' with the peasants, two-thirds of the way lies in lower Rickinghall. More-over the street (a portion of the old turn-pike road from Norwich to Yarmouth) (NB as printed: should read *Bury* to Yarmouth) is not more remarkable for length than for breadth and straightness. In my boyhood this grand way was kept alive, like the narrow streets of Woodbridge, with coaches-and-four and the carriages of grandees, 'travelling post'. In this last respect, the thoroughfare changed strangely for the worse, as the railways shut up the posting houses and drove the coaches from the road: – a sad change for the people who are tied by duty or poverty to the silent and desolate and dolefully dilapidated street!

On coming for the first time to Botesdale, some twenty miles distant from Framlingham, I found myself in novel scenery and a new social atmosphere. Lying in the woodland, but within a few miles of the Fielding, Botesdale was less remarkable than my native district for redun-dancy of foliage and boscage. The hedges were less numerous and high, and the fields four or five times as large as the paddocks and pightels about the town of my birth. The humble people of the district differed notably from the subordinate folk of my proper hundred. Comprising a strikingly large percentage of small men (mere boys in height, though they were grey-haired) with keen countenances and bowed legs, the neighbourhood offered to my boyish consideration fashions of masculine attire that were unfamiliar to me. For headgear the minute bow-legged men preferred a cloth cap, showing the size of the skull; and they wore curiously-cut nether garments of corduroy, extremely baggy about the hips and needlessly tight about the lower parts of the bow-legs. At the same time, the number of horses, whose delicacy of breed and constitution required that they should take their daily walks in clothing, was strikingly great. Had I in that opening stage of my career known aught of Newmarket and Dullingham by personal experience, I should have known that the 'peculiar something' of the Botesdale atmosphere came to it for the most part from Newmarket town and heath. True, 'tis a long call from Botesdale to Newmarket, but the influence of a famous school affects the humour of the country for miles round. From Newmarket to Bury St. Edmunds and from Bury to Wortham the moral and aesthetic tone of the heath was strong in every hamlet and homestead. The social life of Botesdale smacked of the famous racing town.

J. Cordy Jeaffreson, *A Book of Recollections*

15. MILDENHALL

Somehow or other, railways and electric telegraphs, while they have brought most places nearer to the great throbbing centres of commerce and civilisation, have so destroyed the individuality of others as to render objects that were at one time both interesting and instructive mere common-place attractions and every-day sights. Not so, however, in the case of this town. Thanks to the lack of enterprise of a certain well-known railway company, this town, containing over 2000 inhabitants, and the centre of a district with a population of 6000, is without railway accommodation nearer than seven miles, and rejoices in the primitive simplicity represented by carrier's carts and other similar modes of conveyance. Long may it so remain, for a more beautiful and picturesque spot does not exist in the whole of the east of England. It is the capital, so to speak, of quite a cluster of villages and hamlets, all of which rejoice in comparative seclusion from the outer world. It is true that there are railway stations that bear the name of some of them, but by the oddest and happiest arrangements possible, it so happens that they are all several miles distant, while in the case of Mildenhall, there is the exceptionally curious circumstance that the station bearing its name is not the nearest to it by a couple of miles or more. Mildenhall Road, on the Great Eastern Railway, is the station so situated, and like many other stations on the same route, all that can be said of it is that it is on the road to Mildenhall. It is a cruel jest on the part of the booking-clerk at Bishopsgate to hand you a ticket for "Mildenhall Road" when you want to go to Mildenhall; but you have the consolation, when you get to the end of your first stage, of finding out what it is to "Wait for the waggon," and of getting a "cast" in any stray vehicle that may be going towards the town. For you must know that Mildenhall so prides itself at being cut off from the outer world, that it does not encourage visitors by means of the vulgar expedient of the hotel omnibus that "meets every train" and of the night porter who is "always in attendance". Laughable stories are told with immense gusto of commercial travellers who, set down in the middle of a desert, as it were, with quite a ton of samples and luggage, have been constrained to risk the dangerous expedient of "hiring" to the town, only to return the next day with the cruel answer of the indignant tradesmen ringing in their ears, "Nothing wanted today, thank you." It is said that a branch line was once surveyed for; but the surveyor, either being a man of "Mildenhall" himself, or sympathising deeply with the exclusiveness of the people, bungled the survey, and the Bill was thrown out. But who would have a railway to Mildenhall so long as he is free to enjoy the bracing drive from Newmarket across the "Bury hills" and through the delightful avenue of elms that encloses the road for the best part of a couple of miles. Passing the "Half-way House" which is half a road-side inn and half a farm-house, and prides itself upon supplying the best tankard of "home-brewed" in the county, you diverge from the Norwich Road to the left, and glide through the pretty little hamlet of Warlington, with its "village smithy" and the quaint old house of its "oldest residenter". The district is purely agricultural, and the trim farmyards, with their large, well-built and gaily decorated stacks, speak of a season of plenty, as well as of peace. Nothing of Mildenhall is visible till you have quite entered its sacred precincts, except its square Church tower, which is seen distinctly quite a couple of miles away. Rising out of the midst of what appears at a distance a clump of trees, and with that peculiar glint of sunshine upon it which is only experienced now and then in the quiet winter afternoon, it is at once a striking and beautiful object. The town itself, nestled among the trees, and partly surrounded by what must have been intended for a moat, only that there is a stone bridge instead of a drawbridge across it, seems to have been destined by nature to remain the secluded spot it really is. Its old Church, said to be of the 13th or 14th century, and its ancient churchyard, filled with the tombstones of many a "village Hampden", speaks of a time when it must have been the great centre of interest, if not of civilisation itself, to the surrounding country.

A. D. Bayne, *The Illustrated History of Eastern England*

16. EUSTON – A SUFFOLK ESTATE

a) Since first I was at this place, I found things exceedingly improv'd. It is seated in a bottome between two graceful swellings, the maine building being now in the figure of a Greek II with foure pavilions, two at each corner, and a breake in the front, rail'd and balustred at the top, where I caus'd huge jarrs to be plac'd full of earth to keepe them steady upon their pedestalls between the statues, which make as good a shew as if they were of stone, and tho' the building be of brick, and but two stories beside cellars, and garretts cover'd with blue slate, yet there is roome enough for a full court, the offices and out-houses being so ample and well-dispos'd. The King's apartment is painted *à fresca*, and magnificently furnished. There are many excellent pictures of the greate masters. The gallery is a pleasant, noble roome: in the breake, or middle, is a billiard table, but the wainscott being of firr, and painted, does not please me so well as Spanish oake without paint. The chapel is pretty, the porch descending to the gardens. The orange garden is very fine, and leads into the green-house, at the end of which is a hall to eate in, and the conservatory some hundred feete long, adorn'd with mapps, as the other side is with the heads of Caesars ill cut in alabaster: over head are several apartments for my Lord, Lady, and Dutchesse, with kitchens and other offices below in a lesser form, with lodgings for servants, all distinct, for them to retire to when they please and would be in private and have no communication with the palace, which he tells me he will wholly resign to his sonn-in-law and daughter, that charming young creature. The canall running under my lady's dressing-room chamber window is full of carps and foule which come and are fed there. The cascade at the end of the canall turnes a corne-mill, which provides the family, and raises water for the fountaines and offices. To passe this canall into the opposite meadows, Sir Sam. Moreland has invented a screw-bridge, which being turn'd with a key lands you 50 foote distant at the entrance of an ascending walke of trees, a mile in length, as tis also on the front into the park, of 4 rows of ash-trees, and reaches to the park-pale, which is 9 miles in compass, and the best for riding and meeting the game that I ever saw. There were now of red and fallow deere almost a thousand, with good covert, but the soile barren and flying sand, in which nothing will grow kindly. The tufts of firr and much of the other wood were planted by my direction some yeares before. This seate is admirably plac'd for field sports, hawking, hunting, or racing. The mutton is small, but sweete. The stables hold 30 horses and 4 coaches. The out-offices make two large quadrangles, so as servants never liv'd with more ease and convenience, never master more civil. Strangers are attended and accomodated as at their home, in pretty apartments fur nish'd with all manner of conveniences and privacy. There is a library full of excellent books. There are bathing-roomes, elaboratorie, dispensatorie, a decoy, and places to keepe and fat fowl in. He had now in his new church (neere the garden) built a dormitory or vault with several repositories in which to burie his family. In the expence of this pious structure, the church is most laudable, most of the Houses of God in this country resembling rather stables and thatched cottages than temples in which to serve the Most High. He has built a lodge in the park for the keeper, which is a neate dwelling and might become any gentleman. The same has he don for the parson, little deserving it, for murmuring that my Lord put him some time out of his wretched hovel, whilst it was building. He has also erected a faire inn at some distance from his palace, with a bridge of stone over a river neere it, and repaired all the tenants houses, so as there is nothing but neatenesse and accommodations about his estate, which I yet think is not above £1500 a yeare. I believe he had now in his family 100 domestic servants.

John Evelyn, *Diary*

b) We left Newmarket and went on to Euston by Barton Mills. The Bull was very lovely in the September sunlight. Walls newly cream-washed, geraniums blazing in the window-boxes, pigeons cooing on the tiles, a jumble of roofs, chimney-pots, dormer windows, and good, broad, bow windows, white painted, with a vision inside of oak and mahogany, silver and glass. This pub is a perpetual joy to return to. I have memories from 1910 of its stuffed fish, its wildfowl from the Lark in cases – probably shot by old William Howlett in the nineties – and its copper and brass. The Lark was full-bank, swirling under the mill. A trout jumped as we went over the bridge . . .

We went right, by Barnham Heath, another great open warren, criss-crossed by tank tracks, empty of rabbits, musical with stone curlew and peewits. Not a partridge or a pheasant to be seen. But the fir woods on either side were tall and lovely in the afternoon heat-haze. We were in the sandy lands of heath and sighing pines. Miles of rusty bracken and broom, a land empty of house or man, silent in the sun and wind.

As we crossed the invisible boundary on to the Euston property, I could feel somehow an indefinable difference at once. Tidy, white-washed thatched cottages looked very demure, like middle-aged dairymaids. Great elms by the field sides. Rough meadows here and there with cart mares and colts out to grass. No Shires to be seen, but some very nice-looking Suffolk punches. We turned in over the bridge to the stable front of Euston Hall. The house, square, with turrets at either corner, overlooks a narrow lake made by damming up the Little Ouse. Faintly it reminds one of a less ornate, less pretentious Audley End . . .

Euston is a remarkable example of triumph over natural difficulty. The estate includes some of the poorest land in England. Land which, before the war, was almost worthless, fit only to breed rabbits or be let as a pheasant- or partridge-shoot. The Euston land, which Bloomfield, the Suffolk plough-boy poet, knew well and put in such delightful antique verse, is so light that "whole fields hereabout get up and blow away." It is finer than sea sand. It runs through the fingers like sand through an hour-glass. We kicked it up in clouds which whitened us to the knees.

Yet here, on what is probably the poorest land in England, the Duke of Grafton, who farms twelve hundred acres of his fourteen thousand acre estate, has performed miracles. He has reclaimed virgin heathland, where the bracken grew six to eight feet high. In two years he has grown ten sacks of barley to the acre, and ten sacks of rye – "which," he remarked to me, "is more rye than I have ever heard of anywhere." I am inclined to ask if this is not indeed a record.

What the Duke has done at Euston is an object-lesson to every owner of sandy bracken land elsewhere. Norfolk, Hampshire, Dorset, and other counties can show tens of thousands of acres of similar land at present waste.

He began four years before the war by ploughing up five acres of rabbit infested land covered with gorse-bushes. It was horse-ploughed at first, but this was a failure owing to the fibrous mass of roots which extended six to nine inches deep. A tractor ploughing a foot deep was next used. This thoroughly broke the land. Then followed a magnificent crop of marrow-stem kale which was folded off by four hundred ewes for six weeks. The land was then ploughed shallow by tractor, and barley put in. The result was the best barley on the whole farm. The yield was fifty-two sacks to five acres – just over a sack an acre (sic) on almost pure sand, having a chalk subsoil, and with no record of its ever having been ploughed before.

James Wentworth Day, *Farming Adventure*

17. HADLEIGH

Past half-timbered homes of ancient date, and prosperous-looking rick-surrounded farmsteads, whose windows gleamed in the golden light; past old windmills, whose great sails stood out like gigantic outstretched arms darkly silhouetted against the luminous sky; past red-roofed cottages, fragrant with the smell of burning wood, our way led us, till just as the light was fading from land and sky we reached the little town of Hadleigh, and pulled up there before the hospitable door of the ancient and one-time famous White Lion.

Our hostel proved to be a delightful example of the old-fashioned English inn, and the worthy landlord (who told us that he had been there for over twenty-four years) was an excellent specimen of 'mine host' –

civil, obliging, good-natured and chatty. Upon entering this ancient inn we were delightfully surprised to find ourselves in a glass-roofed courtyard, with galleries running around covered with clematis, and here and there were flowers and ferns in pots. Not always does it fall to the lot of the weary traveller to come upon such a pleasant, homely hostel at the end of his day's pilgrimage. In this courtyard, in former times, we were told that the Mystery Plays were performed before large audiences gathered from far and near. At the back of our inn we discovered in the morning a pleasant garden and bowling-green, in which we smoked our after-breakfast pipe and glanced at our guide-book to see what it had to say respecting Hadleigh. We found that it was very full of the past history of the place down to the times of the Saxons, but of the information generally desired by the traveller it contained very little, and some even of that little we afterwards discovered to be wrong.

A charming little countrified town is Hadleigh, full of interesting old houses, many bearing plain evidence of past prosperity, for long years ago Hadleigh was an important seat of the woollen trade. Early in the fourteenth century a large body of Flemings settled here, and to this day the names of the villages around, such as Kersey, Linsey, bear testimony to the former extent of its manufacturing interests by the terms, still retained, that they gave to special products of the loom. And these old Hadleigh merchants built for themselves enduring homes, beautified them with carvings, adorned their fronts with graceful or quaint devices and many a painted legend. They built for permanency in those times, not for a temporary resting place; they sought for beauty too, as well as permanency, cared for it, expected it, obtained it; and though the ancient town has lost its former prosperity, and seems to have fallen into a deep sleep never to waken more, the quaint and picturesque houses still stand, though, alas! some have been more or less damaged by time and others ruined beyond recall by being refronted with little or no feeling for the work of the past.

Yes, in truth a pleasant little town is Hadleigh. I know not a more attractive one, possessing as it does a delightful air of mellowness and old-time calm, so grateful and rare in this busy money-making age. A town it is that has felt less than most such places the levelling influence of nineteenth-century progress, with all its ugliness and slavish uniformity. It is unspoilt by villas, terraces, or residences eligibly situated (with every modern convenience, but inconvenient withal) and shops of stucco and plate-glass are agreeably 'conspicuous by their absence', neither has it any scattered outskirts invading the pleasant green fields around. A more charming town to ramble in there could not be; it is full of interest, and abounds in pictures offering a wealth of subjects for the painter or etcher.

James John Hissey, *A Tour in a Phaeton Through the Eastern Counties*

18. LONG MELFORD

a) The road as far as this town is quite pleasant, especially when one gets near to it, passing through a very long and beautiful village called Melford . . . The village of Melford is built entirely on the main road, which makes it look bigger than it really is. The houses are all well built and there is a noticeable air of comfort. The general scene formed by the patches of green and the various groups of trees and houses is quite delightful, all of them, down to the smallest hovel, being trim and carefully kept. The fences and palings round the houses are all painted white and there are always some flowers to be seen. In a word there is always a marked superiority in the houses of the common people of England over those of the poor peasants of France, which it often pained me to observe.

François de la Rochefoucauld, *A Frenchman in England*

b) "Sure enough you'll never beat the Flaming Tinman in the way you fight – it's of no use flipping at the Flaming Tinman with your left hand; why don't you use your right?"

"Because I'm not handy with it," said I; and then getting up, I once more confronted the Flaming Tinman, and struck him six blows for his one, but they were all left-handed blows, and the blow which the Flaming Tinman gave knocked me off my legs.

"Now, will you use your Long Melford?" said Belle, picking me up.

"I don't know what you mean by Long Melford," said I, gasping for breath.

"Why, this long right of yours," said Belle, feeling my right arm – "if you do, I shouldn't wonder if you yet stand a chance."

. . . At last he aimed a blow, which, had it taken full effect, would doubtless have ended the battle, but owing to his slipping, the fist only grazed my left shoulder, and came with terrific force against a tree, close to which I had been driven; before the tinman could recover himself, I collected all my strength, and struck him beneath the ear, and then fell to the ground completely exhausted, and it so happened that the blow which I struck the Tinker beneath the ear was a right-handed blow.

"Hurrah for Long Melford!" I heard Belle exclaim; "there is nothing like Long Melford for shortness all the world over."

George Borrow, *Lavengro*

19. SUDBURY

a) It was not till I got nearly to Sudbury that I saw much change for the better. Here the bottom of chalk, the soft dirty-looking chalk that the Norfolk people call clay, begins to be the bottom, and this, with very little exception (as far as I have seen) is the bottom of all the lands of these two fine counties of Suffolk and Norfolk. – Sudbury has some fine meadows near it on the sides of the river Stour. The land all along to Bury St Edmund's is very fine; but no trees worth looking at.

William Cobbett, *Rural Rides*

b) Journal of a very young Lady's tour from Canonbury to Aldeburgh . . .
Letter 1. Sudbury, Sep. 13th, 1804

> *At length in good time we're to Sudbury come,*
> *And (thanks to friend M——) have got a good room;*
> *Good lamb, and good ducks, good pye, and good wine;*
> *On which it is soon our intention to dine.*
> *A secret, dear sister, I've now to disclose;*
> *We were join'd, whilst at dinner, by two smart Suffolk beaux;*
> *You may smile, and suppose this is excellent luck,*
> *But one's married, the other's most desp'rately struck;*
> *A rich beautiful cousin of yours and of mine,*
> *This adorable swain thinks completely divine.*
> *We've been strolling an hour, to survey this old town;*
> *One street we walk'd up, another walk'd down;*
> *The barges examin'd, and new navigation,*
> *Not the first in the world, nor the first in the nation;*
> *And are safely return'd, without any affright,*
> *To our snug little inn; and shall stay here all night.*
> *And now we are thinking of supper d'ye see,*
> *So no more at present, my dear sister P.*

James Ford (Ed.), *The Suffolk Garland*

c) On our arrival at Sudbury we had breakfast, and then sent for a manufacturer who told us a little about the trade of the town and about its population. There is one remarkable thing for which the most competent authorities would find it difficult to give a proper account: Why is the population of the towns so different in regard to the class of people who live in them? Why are all classes of people not distributed in each town? Why are some towns inhabited only by the dregs of the people and by

ne'er-do-wells? I must recollect that I am in England, where the nobility
and the gentry, who spend two or three months of the year in the capital,
are evenly distributed through all the counties and round all the towns.
The country round Sudbury is pleasant enough; the hills and valleys
provide agreeable prospects, and yet the town and its neighbourhood are
inhabited only by people without any fortune, by smugglers, bankrupts
and the like. It is a misfortune for which I cannot account, but it is an
established fact that there is not a decent man in the place.

François de la Rochefoucauld, *A Frenchman in England*

20. BURY SAINT EDMUND'S

a) In the town, where rests enshrined Saint Edmund King and Martyr of
glorious memory, Abbot Baldwin held, in King Edward's time, towards
victualling the monks 118 men – and they could give and sell their land –
and under them 52 bordars from whom the Abbot can have some little
aid, 54 free-men poor enough, 43 alms-men each of whom has a bordar. –
Now there are 2 mills. And 2 stews or fishponds. – This town was then
valued at 10 pounds, now at 20. – It is a league and a half in length, and
as much in breadth. – And as often as a pound is paid in the hundred to
the gelt, then there go from the town 60d. to the victualling of the monks.
– But this is from the town as (it was) in the time of King Edward, if so
be; for now the town is contained in a greater circle of land which then
used to be ploughed and seeded: whereon there are 30 what with priests,
deacons and clerks; 28 what with nuns and poor persons who daily utter
prayers for the King and for all Christian people: 80 less five what with
bakers, ale brewers, tailors, washerwomen, shoemakers, cloth workers,
cooks, porters, controllers of household. And all these daily wait upon the
Saint, and the Abbot, and the Brethren.

Entry in Domesday Book

b) So to St. Edmunds-bury 8 mile – but as has been often observed
before the miles are very long – I pass'd by two or 3 little villages and
about 2 mile off there is the town of St. Edmunds Bury which appeares
standing on a great hill; the towers and buildings look so compact and
well together with the trees and gardens thick about it the prospect was
wonderfully pleasant; a mile off by a little village I descended a hill which
made the prospect of the town still in view and much to advantage; its but
two parishes; the Market Cross has a dyal and lanthorn on the top, and
there being another house pretty close to it high built with such a tower
and lanthorn also, with the two churches towers and some other buildings

pretty good made it appear nobly at a distance; this high house is an apothecarys, at least 60 stepps up from the ground and gives a pleaseing prospect of the whole town, that is compact severall streetes but no good buildings; except this the rest are great old houses of timber and mostly in the old forme of the country which are long peaked roofes of tileing; this house is the new mode of building, 4 roomes of a floore pretty sizeable and high, well furnish'd, a drawing roome and chamber full of China and a Damaske bed embroyder'd, 2 other roomes, Camlet and Mohaire beds, a pretty deale of plaite in his wives chamber, parlours below and a large shop; he is esteem'd a very rich man; he shewed me a Curiosity of an Herball all written out with every sort of tree and herb dryed and cut out and pasted on the leaves – it was a Doctor of Physicks work that left it him as Legacy at his death, it was a fine thing and would have delighted me severall dayes but I was passant; there was two streets were broad and very long out of which run a cross 5 or 6 streetes more, which are as good as in most country towns, they were well pitch'd with small stones; there are many Descenters in the town 4 Meeteing places with the Quakers and Anabaptists, there is only the ruines of the Abby walls and the fine gate at the entrance that remaines stone well carv'd; it seemes to be a thriveing industrious town 4 gates in it.

There are a great deale of Gentry which lives in the towne tho' there are no good houses but what are old rambling ones, they are in that they call the Green, a space by the Churches (St. Mary's and St. James') which are pretty near together, they are pretty large but nothing curious in them, stone buildings no monuments worth notice; they keep them very clean and neate and have a moveable scaffold to clean the roofe and windows and walls; its a very dear place so much Company living in the town makes provision scarce and dear, however its a good excuse to raise the reckoning on strangers.

Celia Fiennes, *The Journeys of Celia Fiennes*

c) I shall believe nothing so scandalous of the ladies of this town and the county round it as a late writer insinuates: that the ladies round the country appear mighty gay and agreeable at the time of the fair in this town, I acknowledge; one hardly sees such a show in any part of the world; but to suggest they come hither as a market, is so coarse a jest that the gentlemen that wait on them hither (for they rarely come but in good company) ought to resent and correct him for it.

It is true, Bury Fair, like Bartholomew Fair, is a fair for diversion, more than for trade; and it may be a fair for toys and for trinkets, which the ladies may think fit to lay out some of their money in, as they see occasion. But to judge from thence, that the knights daughters of

Norfolk, Cambridge-shire and Suffolk, that is to say, for it cannot be understood any otherwise, the daughters of all the gentry of the three counties, come hither to be pick'd up, is a way of speaking I never before heard any author have the assurance to make use of in print . . .

But the beauty of this town consists in the number of gentry who dwell in and near it, the polite conversation among them; the affluence and plenty they live in; the sweet air they breathe in, and the pleasant country they have to go abroad in.

Here is no manufacturing in this town, or but very little, except spinning; the chief trade of the place depending upon the gentry who live there, or near it, and who cannot fail to cause trade enough by the expence of their families and equipages, among the people of a county town. They have but a very small river, or rather but a very small branch of a very small river, at this town, which runs from hence to Milden-Hall, on the edge of the Fens. However, the town and gentlemen about, have been at the charge, that they have made this river navigable to the said Milden-Hall, from whence there is a navigable dyke, call'd Milden-Hall Dreyn, which goes into the River Ouse and so to Lynn; so that all their coal and wine, iron, lead and other heavy goods, are brought by water from Lynn, or from London, by the way of Lynn, to the great ease of the tradesmen.

Daniel Defoe, *A Tour Through the Whole Island of Great Britain*

d) To conclude an account of Suffolk and not to sing the praises of Bury St. Edmund's would offend every creature of Suffolk birth; even at Ipswich, when I was praising *that place*, the very people of that town asked me if I did not think Bury St. Edmund's the nicest town in the world. Meet them wherever you will, they all have the same boast; and indeed, as a town *in itself*, it is the neatest place that ever was seen. It is airy, it has several fine open places in it, and it has the remains of the famous abbey walls and the abbey gate entire; and it is so clean and neat that nothing can equal it in that respect. It was a favourite spot in ancient times; greatly endowed with monasteries and hospitals. Besides the famous Benedictine Abbey, there was once a college and a friary; and as to the abbey itself, it was one of the greatest in the kingdom; and was so ancient as to have been founded only about forty years after the landing of Saint Austin in Kent. The land all round about it is good; and the soil is of that nature as not to produce much dirt at any time of the year; but the country about it is *flat*, and not of that beautiful variety that we find at Ipswich.

William Cobbett, *Rural Rides*

The following is the insinuation to which Defoe objected in (c) above!

e) It is famous all over England, not so much for merchandises as for the company. All the neighbouring nobility and gentry come to it every afternoon, as the Duke and Duchess of Grafton, the Lord and Lady Cornwallis, the family of the late Lord Jermyn, many knights and gentlemen of estates, and with them an infinite number of knights' and gentlemen's daughters from Norfolk, Cambridgeshire and Suffolk, who come here to market and that not in vain, for this fair seldom concludes without some considerable matches or intreagues, very advantageous to the knights errant who venture themselves. The diversions of the fair are raffling till it is time to go to the comedy, which is acted every night; which, being ended, the company goes to the Assemblies, which are always in some gentleman's house or other during the fair.

James Howell, *Familiar Letters*

f) In a very little while he began to understand what Archer meant when he talked about the fair. Folk poured into the town in such numbers as Hal had never dreamed of. The Abbot's Bridge was constantly passed and re-passed by the Abbot's people going down to take the tolls, and the stream of merchants, traders, players, jugglers, and men of all sorts, who flocked through the east gate, and stopped, many of them, at the Rose, was never-ending. Hal watched them through his loophole with amazement. Archer, every now and then, came and looked over his shoulder.

"Saw ye ever such a sight?" exclaimed the lad in utter wonder, as a great body of Hans traders came in driving horses and mules piled with furs and goods, and the men, in their strange garments, stood for a while eagerly talking and consulting.

"Ay, there's naught strange to me, save one thing, look you," said Archer uneasily.

"What?"

"Where be the women? Fair time brings them in as thick as crows, wanting furbelows and gimcracks, and this, that and t'other; and here there be scarce any, while for men, there be more than I care to see, and with more look of cloth-yard shafts about them than of fair-traders."

"Tut! there be women."

"Said I there were none? Wherever there's mischief, ye'll find women, look you, as St. Anthony found to his cost. But these be not the sort that come to the fair for pleasure and vanity, and they that come have left their children in their homes."

Archer was manifestly anxious, but Hal troubled himself little about the warder's fears. The day was calm, with flashes of sunshine now and then striking across the greyness, and turning the leaves – already thinned by frost – into brilliant gold. They flashed gaily, too, on the crowd which poured steadily in, on this group after that, on the gaudy dresses of the merry-andrews, the steel points of men-at-arms, the knots of priests and clerics.

Frances Peard, *The Abbot's Bridge*

g) *A STREET AND ITS TRADES: John Lydgate, 'the Monk of Bury', gave a vivid picture of life in his native town in the guise of a portrait of foreign parts.*

> *The streetes paved both in lengthe and bredthe*
> *In checker wyse with stonys white and red,*
> *And every craft that any manner man*
> *In any lond devise or reckon can . . .*
> *Gold-smythes first, and rich jowllers,*
> *And by hem silf crafty browdereris,*
> *Wevers also of wool and of lyne,*
> *Of clothe of gold, damaske, and satyn,*
> *Of welwet, cendel, and double samyt eke,*
> *And every clothe that men list to seke;*
> *Smythes also that could forge wele*
> *Swerdes, pollax, and speries sharp of stele,*
> *Dartes, daggeris, for the mayme and wounde,*
> *And querrel-heds sharp and square y-ground.*
> *There wer also crafty armoureris,*
> *Bowyers, and fast by fletcheris,*
> *And swyche as could make sfates pleyne . . .*

John Lydgate, *Troy Book*

21. IPSWICH

a) The streets of Ipswich, like those of most other ancient towns which have not been destroyed by fire and rebuilt, do not run in right-lines; and therefore do not strike a stranger's eye, as they would if they were more regular; but they contain many good houses, which generally are better within, than their outward appearance gives reason to expect. One favourable circumstance is almost peculiar to this place, which is that most of the better houses, even in the heart of the town, have convenient gardens adjoining to them, which make them more airy and healthy, as well as more pleasant and delightful.

The many walks and rides which abound with a variety of pleasing views, together with the goodness of the roads in the environs of Ipswich, do also contribute greatly towards making the place agreeable. But however entertaining these prospects on the land may be, they are far exceeded by those that the Orwell affords; which, to speak cautiously, at least for the extent of it, is one of the most beautiful salt rivers in the world. The beauty of it arises chiefly from its being bounded with highland on both sides, almost the whole way. These hills on each side are enriched and adorned with almost every object that can make a landscape agreeable; such as churches, mills, gentlemen's seats, villages and other buildings, woods, noble avenues, parks whose pales reach down to the water's edge, well stored with deer and other cattle, feeding in fine lawns etc etc. all these and more are so happily disposed and diversified, as if Nature and Art had jointly contrived how they might most agreeably entertain and delight the eye. Such are the side views. As a passenger sails from Ipswich, when he enters what is properly called Orwell Haven, the scene terminates on the right with a view of Harwich and the high coast of Essex; on the left with Landguard Fort, and the high land of Walton and Felixstow Cliffs behind it; and with a prospect of the main ocean before him. As he returns to Ipswich, the scene closes with a distinct view of that fair town, displaying itself to some advantage, and forming a sort of half-moon as the river winds.

John Kirby, *The Suffolk Traveller*

b) The town is badly built, the streets are narrow and irregularly laid out, and the surface of the roads is as bad as it can be. As England is short of stone, such roads in the towns as are made, are made of pebbles packed together; these offer sharp points to the feet and are as uncomfortable when you are riding in a carriage as when you are walking.

The town has a deserted air, and you see hardly anyone in the streets. This is in some small measure due to its extent being much increased by the large number of gardens within its boundaries. It is claimed that this adds to the healthiness of the place. Ipswich is very well populated: many gentlefolk reside there as well as the traders. Every evening they all assemble in a café, which is very convenient for strangers.

As to the trade of the place, I was told that it was considerable. It consists in the export of the products of the countryside to London and to the North. The vessels engaged in this latter export trade bring back planks of fir, which are extensively used for the staircases and floors of houses; they also bring back other products of the North.

Mr. Young knew a man in the town whom we went to see. He was a gentleman-farmer, that is to say, a man who cultivates his farm himself. His land is in a most agreeable position on Stock Hill, east of the town.

From one side of it there is a view of the whole of the bay of which I have already spoken in connection with Mr. Berners' house; from the other you see the town at your feet and three valleys which meet together, each having a little winding stream. It is a delightful position . . .

There is another place from which an even better view of the town and its surroundings is obtained, namely a priory. The fine house and park belong in fact to an aged ecclesiastic, but he is not a prior. From there you get a much better view of the town, for although it is at your feet, it stretches out further and the countryside strikes you from this point as having a more joyous air.

It is a very remarkable thing that at Ipswich, which is a large town and the capital of a large county, there is not a single inn that is even passable; whereas generally you find them in unpretentious villages to be quite excellent and lacking in nothing – not even in cleanliness.

François de la Rochefoucauld, A Frenchman in England

c) In the main street of Ipswich, on the left-hand side of the way, a short distance after you have passed through the open space fronting the Town Hall, stands an inn known far and wide by the appellation of The Great White Horse, rendered the more conspicuous by a stone statue of some rampacious animal with flowing mane and tail, distinctly resembling an insane cart-horse, which is elevated above the principal door. The Great White Horse is famous in the neighbourhood, in the same degree as a prize ox, or county paper-chronicled turnip, or unwieldy pig – for its enormous size. Never were such labyrinths of uncarpeted passages, such clusters of mouldy, ill-lighted rooms, such huge numbers of small dens for eating or sleeping in, beneath any one roof, as are collected together between the four walls of the Great White Horse at Ipswich.

Charles Dickens, The Pickwick Papers

d) There is a great deal of very good company in this town, and though there are not so many of the gentry here as at *Bury*, yet there are more here than in any other town in the county, and I observed particularly that the company you meet with here are generally persons well informed of the world and who have something very solid and entertaining in their society; this may happen, perhaps, by their frequent conversing with those who have been abroad, and by their having a remnant of gentlemen and masters of ships among them, who have seen more of the world than people of an inland town are likely to have seen. I take this town to be one of the most agreeable places in *England*, for families who have lived well but may have suffered in our late calamities of stocks and bubbles, to retreat to, where they may live within their own compass, and several things indeed recommend it to such:

1. Good houses at very easy rents.
2. An airy, clean and well governed town.
3. Very agreeable and improving company almost of every kind.
4. A wonderful plenty of all manner of provisions, whether flesh or fish, and very good of the kind.
5. Those provisions very cheap, so that a family may live cheaper here than in any town in *England* of its bigness, within such a small distance from *London*.
6. Easy passage to *London*, either by land or water, the coach going through to *London* in a day.

Daniel Defoe, *A Particular and Diverting Account of Whatever is Curious*

e) A town without inhabitants, a river without water, streets without names, and where the asses wore boots.

    George Villiers, Second Duke of Buckingham (To King Charles II)

f) What I have said, is only to let the world see, what improvement this town and port is capable of; I cannot think, but that Providence, which made nothing in vain, cannot have reserv'd so useful, so convenient a port to lie vacant in the world, but that the time will some time or other come (especially considering the improving temper of the present age) when some peculiar beneficial business may be found out, to make the port of Ipswich as useful to the world, and the town as flourishing, as nature had made it proper and capable to be.

As for the town, it is true, it is but thinly inhabited, in comparison of the extent of it; but to say, there are hardly any people to be seen there, is far from being true in fact; and whoever thinks fit to look into the churches and meeting-houses on a Sunday, or other publick days, will find there are very great numbers of people there: Or if he thinks fit to view the market, and see how the large shambles, call'd Cardinal Wolsey's Butchery, are furnish'd with meat, and the rest of the market stock'd with other provisions, much acknowledge that it is not for a few people that all those things are provided: A person very curious, and on whose veracity I think I may depend, going thro' the market in this town, told me, that he reckon'd upwards of 600 country people on horseback and on foot, with baskets and other carriage, who had all of them brought something or other to town to sell, besides the butchers, and what came in carts and waggons.

It happen'd to be my lot to be once at this town, at the time when a very fine new ship, which was built there, for some merchants of London, was to be launched; and if I may give my guess at the numbers of people which appeared on the shore, in the houses, and on the river I believe I am much within compass, if I say there were 20,000 people to see it; but this is only a guess, or they might come a great way to see the sight, or the town may be declin'd farther since that: But a view of the town is one of the surest rules for a gross estimate.

It is true, here is no settled manufacture: the French refugees, when they first came over to England, began a little to take to this place; and some merchants attempted to set up a linnen manufacture in their favour; but it has not met with so much success as was expected, and at present I find very little of it. The poor people are however employ'd, as they are all over these counties, in spinning wool for other towns where manufactures are settled.

Daniel Defoe, *A Tour Through the Whole Island of Great Britain*

g) It is a very neat and well built town, much larger than many cities, and well filled with gentry and other inhabitants. It was formerly famous for the manufactures of broad-cloth, and the best canvas for sailcloth, called Ipswich double; it has had several companies of traders, incorporated by charters, as clothiers, merchant taylors, merchant adventurers etc. It has a very spacious market place, in the midst of which is a fair cross, in which is the corn market: adjoining to this is the Shambles, or butchery, which is very commodious, commonly supposed to have been built by Cardinal Wolsey; but this I find to be a mistake, for that it was built long since, that is, towards the end of the reign of Queen Elizabeth, for in her 40th year, Nov. 16, there is an order of Court for a committee to build the butchery, and to cut down and carry timber for it from the Copyhold Estate at Ulverstone. Behind this is the Herb Market. There is also a large market for butter, poultry, and other country provisions, in a spacious street a little distant from this; and another for fish, with which the town is served in great plenty.

John Kirby, *The Suffolk Traveller* (Ist Ed.)

h) But about the middle of the last century the manufactory began to decline; and then dwindled by degrees, till at last it totally ceased. The loss of the manufactory was attended with bad effects. We must suppose the principal artificers would follow the trade into the north and west part of the Kingdom, where it has settled ever since. But vast numbers of the poorer sort employed in it, were left behind; and these, when their employment ceased, became a burden and incumberance to the town and neighbourhood. This might very probably be one reason which prevented other persons from settling here, in the room of those who followed the manufactory. From hence it happened, that very many of the better sort of houses were for a long while empty; and Ipswich incurred the censure of being a *town without people*. But now, the case is otherwise. The inconvenience before-mentioned abated, and wore out in time. The agreeableness of the town invited new-comers to settle here; and the number of inhabitants is so much increased, that within fifty years the rents are advanced more than fifty per cent, almost every house is full, and more houses are daily wanted. Insomuch that it is difficult to procure one that will accommodate a middling family; all such being in a manner scrambled for.

John Kirby, *The Suffolk Traveller* (2nd Ed.)

i) So I went to Ipswitch 9 mile more, this is a very clean town and much bigger than Colchester is now, Ipswitch has 12 churches, their streetes of a good size well pitch'd with small stones, a good Market Cross railed in, I was there on Satturday which is their market day and saw they sold their butter by the pinte, 20 ounces for 6 pence, and often for 5d. or 4d. they make it up in a mold just in the shape of a pinte pot and so sell it; their Market Cross has good carving, the figure of Justice carv'd and gilt, there is but 3 or 4 good houses in the town, the rest is much like the Colchester buildings but it seems more shatter'd, and indeed the town looks a little disregarded, and by enquiry found it to be thro' pride and sloth, for tho' the sea would bear a ship of 300 tun up quite to the key and the ships of the first rate can ride within two mile of the town, yet they make no advantage thereof by any kind of manufacture, which they might do as well as Colchester and Norwitch, so that the shipps that brings their coales goes light away; neither do they address themselves to victual or provide for shipps, they have a little dock where formerly they built ships of 2 or 300 tun but now little or nothing is minded save a little fishing for the supply of the town.

Celia Fiennes, *The Journeys of Celia Fiennes*

j) To divert me, my Lord would needs carry me to see Ipswich, when we din'd with one Mr. Mann by the way, who was Recorder of the towne. There were in our company my Lord Huntingtoure sonn to the Dutchesse of Lauderdale, Sir Ed. Bacon a learned gentleman of the family of the greate Chancellor Verulam, and Sir John Felton, with some other Knights and Gentlemen. After dinner came the Bailiff and Magistrates in their formalities with their maces to compliment my Lord and invite him to the Towne-house, where they presented us a collation of dried sweet meates and wine, the bells ringing etc. Then we went to see the towne, and first, the Lord Viscount Hereford's house, which stands in a park neere the towne, like that at Bruxelles in Flanders; the house is not greate yet pretty, especially the hall. The stewes for fish succeed one another and feed one the other, all paved at bottome. There is a good picture of the *Bl. Virgin* in one of the parlours, seeming to be of Holbein or some good master. Then we saw the Haven, 7 miles from Harwich. The tide runs out every day, but the bedding being soft mudd it is safe for shipping and a station. The trade of Ipswich is for the most part Newcastle coales, with which they supply London, but it was formerly a cloathing towne. There is not any beggar asks alms in the whole place, a thing very extraordinary, so order'd by the prudence of the Magistrates. It has in it 14 or 15 beautiful churches: in a word 'tis for building, cleanesse, and good order, one of the best townes in England. Cardinal Wolsey was a butcher's sonn of this towne, but there is little of that magnificent Prelate's foundation here, besides a schole and I think a library, which I did not see. His intentions were to build some greate thing. We return'd late to Euston, having travell'd above 50 miles this day.

John Evelyn, *Diary*

Debate on the future of Ipswich as an industrial or commercial centre of an expanding region is clearly not new: although the proponents of this particular scheme for a Mart at Ipswich, had they won their way, may well have ended up with Ipswich as a Europort (on the Rotterdam pattern) several centuries ago!

k) So the devisers doe inferre hereapon, howe for gayne and bye good governement, the Countrye of Englande all about the said marte towne of Ipsewiche and farther of bye industrye and tyme, will or maye in reason growe full of making of all lynnen commoditie, new draperye of wullen and lynnen, and of all other store of manuell occupacons, walled townes, villags, and buildings, maryners, saylers, fishermen, and shipping, welthe, monye and all necessaryes whatsoever that the lowe Countryes hath at this daye or ever had before, when it was most flowrishing . . .
Against (*i.e. the drawbacks to this attractive scheme*)
The scituacon of Ipsewiche is not soe safe against invasion bye sea as Andwarp is, being more distannt from the sea, and having flusshinge a

stronge towne bye the waye, to withstand souche invaders, and though the mouthe of Ipsewiche ryver on Harwich syde and on Suff syde, maye be made stronge bye fortes and bulwarkes, and bye watche daye and night, yet the charge thereof wilbe greate and muche must be bestowed at the begynning, and more must bee yearlye fasshioned, to finishe souche strength against all sodeyne invasion, that the merchaunts to bee intised thither, may see theire goodes, wilbe aswell safe as without imposicon, and as redye to bee bought as before at Andwarpe, and whoe shall begynne this first charge is the matter.

Ipswich a Mart for General Traffic, from 'Suffolk Notes'

l) *Queen Elizabeth I visited Ipswich in July, 1561.* Here, her Majesty took a great dislike to the imprudent behaviour of many of the ministers and readers, there being many weak ones amongst them, and little or no order observed in the public service, and few or none wearing the surplice. And the Bishop of Norwich was thought remiss, and that he winked at schismatics. But more particularly was she offended with the clergy's marriage: and that in cathedral colleges there were so many wives and widows and children seen, which she said was contrary to the interest of the founders, and so much tending to the interruption of the studies of those who are placed there. Therefore she issued an order to all dignitaries, dated August 9th at Ipswich, to forbid all women to the lodgings of cathedralls or colleges, and that upon pain of losing their ecclesiastical promotions.

John Strype, *Life of Matthew Parker*

m) *The following letter is in MS in the British Museum: dated 27 May 1836, and sent to Mrs. Charles Dickens. It provides a graphic illustration of the way Dickens utilised his experience as a reporter at Ipswich to provide background for the work on which he was then engaged,* The Pickwick Papers.

Suffolk Hotel, Ipswich.

My dear Kate,

I shall be home please God, to dinner tomorrow at *half past five*, as I have booked my place by the coach which leaves here at 9 in the morning. We arrived here about 5; the night was cold, but beautifully fine, and the ride upon the whole was a very pleasant one, the more especially as the mode of conveyance enabled us to partake of a good supper on the road. It is now half past one, and huge mobs are assembled to greet OConnell who is every moment expected. From the appearance of the crowd, and the height of party feeling here, I rather expect a Row . . .

Charles Dickens

n) Mr. Pickwick and Mr. Tupman squeezed themselves inside, and pulled down the blinds; a couple of chairmen were speedily found; and the procession started in grand order. The specials surrounded the body of the vehicle; Mr. Grummer and Mr. Dubbley marched triumphantly in front; Mr. Snodgrass and Mr. Winkle walked arm-in-arm behind; and the unsoaped of Ipswich brought up the rear.

The shopkeepers of the town, although they had a very indistinct notion of the nature of the offence, could not but be much edified and gratified by this spectacle. Here was the strong arm of the law, coming down with twenty gold-beater force, upon two offenders from the metropolis itself; the mighty engine was directed by their own magistrate, and worked by their own officers; and both the criminals by their united efforts, were securely shut up, in the narrow compass of one sedan-chair. Many were the expressions of approval and admiration which greeted Mr. Grummer, as he headed the cavalcade, staff in hand; loud and long were the shouts raised by the unsoaped; and amidst these united testimonials of public approbation, the procession moved slowly and majestically along.

Charles Dickens, *The Pickwick Papers*

o) Ipswich in 1910 was a rough, tough town. One did not venture into the populous parts on a Saturday night because of the drunks who were often to be found lying insensible in the gutter. In 1910 the Lloyd George 'Two acres and a cow' election, so called because of his proposal to create a large system of small holdings, was bitterly contested. The shutters were up in the main streets and the town looked as if it was in a state of siege.

Even in the daytime one could, in the poorer areas of the town, see much drunkenness. I, as a small boy, was privileged to witness a magnificent example of this.

One day, scudding along the street, I was attracted by the shrill noise of shrieks and falsetto curses, and turning the corner I saw on the opposite pavement two women outside a public house. They fought each other clawing, scratching and shrieking like tiger cats. Both had long raven-black hair which tumbled down over their backs and shoulders. Both wore nothing but a thin white nightdress and both were barefooted as if they had just got out of bed. At one moment the stouter of the two dragged her opponent along the pavement by her hair. The next moment the thin one retaliated by tearing away the front of the other's night gown, leaving her heavy breasts and most of her belly exposed.

Over the engraved glass which covered the lower half of the public bar window the heads of men could be seen watching them. The only other spectators were a small boy and a tiny, ragged girl.

Edward Ardizzone, *The Young Ardizzone*

p) Phoebe Lockwood talking about butter enticed me into a long digression on labour and employers. This is not as completely irrelevant as it may seem because I went from rural Eye to the great industrial town of Ipswich. Cobbett found it a beautiful town with about twelve thousand inhabitants, surrounded by cornfields, with windmills grinding vast quantities of flour for London. Wheat at Ipswich, he said, was often worth six shillings a quarter more than at Norwich, 'the navigation to London being so much more speedy and safe.'

I came to Ipswich, which is still a beautiful town, but now has one hundred thousand inhabitants instead of Cobbett's twelve thousand. I fear many of the fields, meadows and white farm-houses must have been swallowed up, and certainly the windmills have gone. There may be one still working but I did not see it in all my travels. There were a few in reasonable preservation and still fewer with skeleton sails remaining, but what remains is only a praiseworthy, sentimental attempt to save the old look of the countryside. Once grain started to flow in a flood from the American prairies the obvious place for mills was at a few ports rather than in a thousand villages. The very big port mills could install machinery impossible for the country miller, and the rather fantastic position arose that English wheat was carted to the port mills to be ground.

Cobbett saw the port of Ipswich as a place from which Suffolk flour was sent to London. The port is still here, indeed sailing barges still make the journey, for I saw three being towed out of the docks by one barge with power. But the cargoes are not all flour for London, they may come from London with flour for Ipswich . . .

Ralph Wightman, *Rural Rides* (After Cobbett)

VI. CUSTOMS, FOLK LORE AND CURIOSITIES

1. CURIOSITIES IN SUFFOLK

(*The curiosity being the corroborative detail in an otherwise bald narrative!*)

Ipswich, the chief town of this county, is noted for a good free-school, and library, as also for its cleanness, and spaciousness. It hath an harbour, 12 parish churches and good gates; 'tis about 55 miles from London.

Hemingston, is remarkable for what is said of one, who held lands there by serjeantry of the Crown, and was obliged every Christmas Day to Dance, make a noise with his cheeks puffed out and let a F--t before the King, 'tis about 5 miles N. from Ipswich.

Framlingham Castle, is very beautiful, fortified with a rampier, ditch and strong wall. 'Tis about 11 miles N.E. from Ipswich.

Orford, At this place the fishermen catched in their net a Sea-Man, who had all the parts of a man, with hair, beard etc. But in a short time he made his escape to sea again. 'Tis about 10 miles near E. from Ipswich.

Printed by Sam Illidge, *British Curiosities in Art and Nature*

2. SUFFOLK WILES

Essex Stiles, Kentish miles,
Suffolk wiles, many men beguiles

Suffolk is said to have been remarkable for ligation and the quirks and quibbles of its attorneys: this was so great a grievance in the reign of Henry VI that, AD 1455, a petition was presented from the Commons, shewing that the number of attornies for the counties of Suffolk and Norfolk had lately increased from 6 or 8 to 80, whereby the peace of those counties had been greatly interrupted by suits. They therefore petitioned it might be ordained, that there should be no more than six common attornies for the county of Suffolk ... The King granted the petition, provided it was thought reasonable by the judges.

James Ford, *Note in the Suffolk Garland*

3. THE WITCH-FINDER

Hopkins is represented in an old engraving as a spare man with a tight-fitting dress, conical hat, and a staff in his hand. He first visited Aldeburgh the day before the execution of an old woman, Mother Lakeland, at

Ipswich, on the 8th September 1645, who, in a pamphlet published after her death, is said to have confessed that she had sold herself to the devil twenty years before, and had been furnished with three imps, in the forms of two dogs and a mole, by which she had grievously afflicted Mr. Lawrence, Mr. Beal, a maid of Mr. Jennings's, besides other persons in that town.

The following items from the Chamberlain's accounts for 1645–6 will best narrate Hopkins's activity at Aldeburgh:–

"Given Mr. Hopkyns, the 8th September, £2 for a gratuitie, he being in town for finding out witches. One pound to Goody Phillips there for her pains for searching out witches. 13s 10d. to sundry men for watching days and nights with such as are apprehended for witches. Two pounds more to Mr. Hopkins, the 20th December, for being in town for finding out witches. One pound to widow Phillips, the search-woman. 12s. 8d. paid Mr. Thos. Johnson, that he paid Mr. Skinner's men for fetching widow Phillips. A further sum of £2 for Mr. Hopkyns for a gratuitie for giving evidence against the witches in the jail, the 7th of January . . . Paid John Pame, eleven shillings for hanging seven witches. Paid Mr. Dannell, £1 for the gallows and setting them up . . . Paid Henry Lawrence, the roper, eight shillings for seven halters, and making the knots.

N. F. Hele, *Notes or Jottings About Aldeburgh*

4. His Method

Matthew Hopkins assumed the title of Witch-finder General, and travelling through the counties of Essex, Sussex, Suffolk, Norfolk, and Huntingdon, pretended to discover witches . . . His principal mode of discovery was to strip the accused persons naked and thrust pins into various parts of their body, to discover the witch's mark, which was supposed to be inflicted by the devil as a sign of his sovereignty, and at which she was also said to suckle her imps. He also practised and stoutly defended the trial by swimming, when the suspected person was wrapped in a sheet, having the great toes and thumbs tied together, and so dragged through a pond or river. If she sank, it was received in favour of the accused; but if the body floated (which must have occurred ten times for once, if it was placed with care on the surface of the water) the accused was condemned, on the principle of King James, who, in treating of this mode of trial, lays down that, as witches have renounced their baptism, so it is just that the element through which the holy rite is enforced should reject them, which is a figure of speech, and no argument. It was Hopkins's custom to keep the poor wretches waking, in order to prevent them from having encouragement from the devil, and, doubtless, to put infirm, terrified, overwatched persons in the next state of absolute madness; and for the same purpose they were dragged about by their keepers till extreme weariness and the pain of blistered feet might form additional inducements to confession.

Sir Walter Scott, *Demonology and Witchcraft*

5. ITS POPULARITY

There was a great crowd in the kitchen of the village inn, the evening after the men had been to the Hall to complain of Mrs. Figgins. The landlord sat beaming to see all the farmers come in, the pack-man, and tea-man, Jack o' Flarey, and many others, who all had soon before them large brown mugs of beer. The long low room was a striking picture of old Suffolk life, the whitewashed walls had pictures in black frames, of horses belonging to the old squire, and a work of art in woollen tapestry, showing David cutting off Goliath's head, and this had been worked by the mother of the landlord; who never saw that there was a Suffolk cottage and homestead in the background. In the open fire-place was a large bunch of lilac and wallflowers. After the brown mugs had been half emptied and set down on the table with loud smacks from the lips of the drinkers, Farmer Drone stood up and knocked on the table to show they must be quiet; then he said 'Look you here, all on you. My masters! we aint a going for to be tret no longer like warment! the squre won't do nothing, du he think we care a brass button for him! That ould witch Figgins shall be punished. W'ill try her in the big pond an' see if she swim!' A loud shout of joy came from all at this, and one after another told of how they had suffered by the bewitching of cattle or children, etc. etc. Louder and louder grew the noise, the landlord filled all the mugs again and called out 'Look you hare! She ha' run two cows o' mine dry! she have, drottle her!' At this a voice came from the end of the room, 'yow din't giv' um' enough to ate, that cum of starving they! I sar she han't nothin' for to du along on they going dry!' But great was the anger at this speech, and the old man got out of the room as soon as he could.

A loud voice now cried 'Look you here, folks all! I tell you I ha' sin the ould witch fly out on her chimley on her broomstick, as plain as a pike-staff I did.' But the tea-man called out 'Why! man I say that's all my eye! you only see a bustard go flying over her cottage, I see a big flock of them the other day, they look very queer when they go flying.' But no one believed the tea-man – what should he know about Suffolk! and so it was settled that they would punish the witch by trial in the water as soon as they could. Jack o' Flarey heard all the plans, and he pretended to agree.

Very soon Jack was sitting in Mrs. Figgins' cottage, where in confidence he told her of the danger she was in, and said 'never fare, mother, you've hope we a lot, and we'll stan' by yow, I'll ha' my ears open, an' the gang woll find a way to hide you! Royston's off before long, and he can take you along of him over the sea.

Now came the day for the execution of the prisoners. Roselands village was in great commotion, but the town looked like fair-time, a crowd was round the prison, and they rent the air with shouts, and singing rough songs. The constables tried in vain to quiet them. They shouted 'Hood you! we wool du as we du, du! We sholl never ha' such a sight agin. The ould Methodys be a'coming for to shut up all the Public Housen.' A loud yell of rage burst from the mob at this speech, and the tumult grew worse and worse.

At last all was over! night came, and a heavy rain dispersed the wild mob, and no sound was heard but the distant moaning of the sea.

Lois A. Fison, *Spinning Days and Olden Ways*

6. The Little Green People of Woolpit

It chanced one day that I was walking in the country and not far from the town of Stowmarket. The time of year was winter and the time of day was evening, when I came upon a little dip of land that led on to a little valley and a little stream and a little fringe of woodland. The scenery as in all Suffolk was not particularly striking and it was nowhere grand, but there was a subtle quality in it, a quality of compelling charm that led me on from point to point in anticipation of something indefinable.

The path that I had chosen was a field track and no road, and soon I came upon a windmill. The breeze was light, blowing from the west, the sails were sweeping round in that solemn silence that only a windmill can give to human activity. Across the valley, where through the trees I could see the silver ribbon of a stream, rose well-wooded land now showing as a blue background.

Still keeping along the edge of the higher land I came upon a curious hole in the ground at the edge of which stood a pollard tree, the sort of place I thought would be a good setting for a scene of little brown men coming up from their busy underworld. I wondered if the county people of Suffolk still believe in Pixies and fairies and witches. I have been told that some of them do and I must say if ever little green people could become realities it would be in such a place as this.

Donald Maxwell, *Unknown Suffolk*

7. SUFFOLK MARVELS

These three marvels come from a small collection of local miracles added to Ralph of Coggeshall's English Chronicle (Chronicon Anglicanum) at some time in the mid-thirteenth century.

Of a certain wild man caught in the sea.

In the time of Henry II, when Bartholomew de Glanville was keeper of Orford castle, it happened that fishermen fishing in the sea there caught a wild man in their nets; who was taken to the aforesaid castellan as a marvel. He was entirely naked, and like a human being in all his limbs. But he had hair, though it seemed on the surface almost torn away and destroyed. His beard was full and pointed, and his chest was extremely hairy and shaggy. The aforesaid knight had him guarded day and night for a long time, so that he could not approach the sea. Whatever was brought to him he ate greedily. He ate fish raw as well as cooked, but he wrung out the raw fish in his hands, until all the liquid had gone, and then ate them. But he would not utter a word, or rather could not, even though he was hung up by his feet, and often severely tortured. When he was taken to a church, he showed not the least sign of reverence or belief, either by kneeling or bowing his head, when he saw anything holy He always hurried to his sleeping place at nightfall and slept there until dawn. It happened that they took him once to the harbour and let him loose in the sea, having placed a triple line of very strong nets across the harbour. He soon made for the depths of the sea, passing all the nets, and repeatedly came up from the deep water, gazing at those who were watching him from the shore for a long time, often diving down and reappearing after a moment, as though he was mocking those who watched him because he had escaped from their nets. He played like this in the sea for a long while, and everyone had given up hope that he would return, but he came back of his own accord to them, swimming through the waves, and remained with them for another two months. But after this he was less carefully guarded, and he now disliked his way of life; so he secretly slipped down to the sea and never appeared again. Whether this was a mortal man or some kind of fish pretending to be a human being or some evil spirit lurking in the body of a drowned man (such as is described in the life of St Audoen) it is not easy to see, particularly because so many people tell such marvellous tales about this kind of event.

Of a certain boy and girl who came up out of the ground.

Another wonderful event not unlike the first happened in Suffolk at St Mary Woolpit. A certain boy and his sister were found by the inhabitants of that place near the mouth of a certain cave there; their limbs and bodies were like those of other men, but they were different in the colour of their skin from all men who live in our country, because the whole of the surface of their skin was green in colour. No-one could understand their language. They were therefore taken to the house of a certain knight called Richard de Calne at Wix, as a marvel; but they wept inconsolably. Bread and other food was brought to them, but they would not eat anything that was offered, even though they were undoubtedly suffering from great hunger through fasting, because they thought that all these kinds of food were inedible, as the girl later admitted. However, when newly-harvested beans still on their stalks were brought to the house, they eagerly asked to be given some. When the beans were brought, they opened the stalks, not the pods, thinking that they would find beans in the hollow of the stalks; but when they found nothing there, they began to weep again. The bystanders saw this and opened the pods, showing them the naked beans; and they ate these very cheerfully, hardly touching any other food for a long while. The boy, however, grew languid and depressed, and died soon afterwards. The girl continued to flourish and, getting used to all kinds of food, gradually lost her leek-green colour and recovered a normal flesh and blood appearance over her whole body. She was later baptised, and stayed for many years in the service of the aforesaid knight, as we frequently heard from the knight and his family;* and she was always extremely playful and wanton. She was often asked about the people of her country, and declared that everyone who lived there and everything in that country was green, and that they never saw the sun, but enjoyed the kind of light that occurs after twilight. Asked how she arrived in this world with the boy, she said that when they were following their flocks, they went into a certain cave. There they heard a delightful noise of bells; enchanted by its sweetness, they wandered through the cave for a long time until they came out of it. When they emerged, they were frightened and almost fainted because of the brightness of the sun and the unaccustomed warmth of the air; and they remained for a long time at the mouth of the cave. When they were terrified by the approach of people, they wanted to escape, but were unable to find the entrance of the cave again, and so were captured.

Of a certain fantastic spirit

In king Richard's time, at Dagworth in Suffolk, in the house of Sir Osbern de Bradwell, a certain fantastic spirit appeared on many occasions over a period of time, speaking to the knight's family with the voice of a

---

*William of Newburgh, who tells the same story with minor differences, says that she married and went to live at King's Lynn. He also adds that the bells heard by the children was those of Bury St Edmunds.

one year old child, and calling itself Malkin. It said that its mother and brother lived in a nearby house, and as, so it said, they often scolded it, it preferred to leave them and go and talk to men. It both behaved and talked in an extraordinary and laughable way, sometimes revealing actions which no-one else could have seen. At first the knight's wife and the whole household were terrified by its talking, but afterwards they got used to its words and ridiculous doings, and talked to it confidently and familiarly, asking it many questions. It spoke English with a local accent, and sometimes Latin, and argued about the Scriptures with the knight's chaplain, and he himself has assured us that this is true. It could be heard and understood, but never seen; except on one occasion when a certain maidservant saw it in the shape of a very small child clothed in a white tunic, and that was only because the girl asked and adjured it to make itself visible. It refused to grant her request unless the girl swore by Our Lord not to touch it or hold it. It said that it was born at Lancham. When its mother took it with her into the fields, where she was harvesting with others, she left it alone in a corner of the field and another woman carried it off and it had now been with her for seven years; after another seven years, it said, it would return to its original human dwelling-place. It said that it and others used a certain cloak, which made them invisible. It often demanded food and drink from bystanders; when this was placed on a certain chest, neither food nor drink was found again.

Ralph of Coggeshall, English Chronicle

8. Wizard Winter

The most famous man in these parts as a wizard was old Winter of Ipswich. My father was in early life apprentice to him and after that was servant to Major Whyte who lived in Stowupland at Sheepgate Hall. A farmer lost some blocks of wood from his yard and consulted Winter about the thief. By mutual arrangement Winter spent the night at the farmer's house, and set the latter to watch, telling him not to speak to anybody he saw. About twelve a labourer living near came into the wood-yard and hoisted a block on his shoulder. He left the yard and entered the meadow, out of which lay a style into his own garden. And when he got into the field he could neither find the style nor leave the field. And round and round the field he had to march with the heavy block on his shoulder, affrighted, yet not able to stop walking, until ready to die with exhaustion, the farmer and Winter watching him from the window, until from pure compassion Winter went up to him, spoke, dissolved the charm, and relieved him from his load.

A. G. H. Hollingsworth, History of Stowmarket

9. A WITCH'S WORK

At St. Edmund's Bury in Suffolk, Sept. 6, 1660, in the middle of the Broad Street, there were got together an innumerable company of Spiders of a redish colour, the spectators judged them to be so many as would have filled a Peck; these Spiders marched together and in a strange kind of order, from the place where they were first discovered, towards one Mr. Duncomb's house, a member of the late Parliament, and since Knighted; and as the people passed the street, or came near the spiders, to look upon so strange a sight, they would shun the people, and kept themselves together in a body till they came to the said Duncomb's house, before whose door there are two great Posts, there they staied, and many of them got under the door into the house, but the greatest part of them, climbing up the posts, spun a very great web presently from the one post to the other, and then wrapt themselves in it in two very great parcels that hung down near to the ground, which the servants of the house at last perceiving, got dry straw and laid it under them, and putting fire to it by a suddain flame consumed the greatest part of them, the number of those that remained were not at all considerable; all the use that the Gentleman made of this strange accident, so far as we can learn, is only this, that he believes they were sent to his house by some witches.

S. Tymms (Ed.), *East Anglian or: Notes and Queries Vol III*

10. HIGH HOUSE, OULTON

On reaching Oulton, a large structure called the High House at once attracts the rambler's attention, from its pleasant situation and dilapidated condition. It stands at the corner of the road, and has long been a theme of wonder to the lovers of the marvellous, for this is a "haunted house". Many versions of the story are told, but all agree that a murder has to do with it. One is that periodically a figure mounted on a coal-black horse, with fiery eyes and expanded nostrils, followed by a pack of yelping dogs with foaming mouths, dashes through the front door and vanishes into the adjoining room. This is the squire who murdered his wife, Another is that a female figure "walks" every night at twelve, habited in white, carrying a cup in her hand. This is the wife who poisoned the squire, and is condemned to walk and have the instrument of her guilt constantly before her ... In truth, all around is a strange neighbourhood, abounding in quaint story and ancient legend, affording fit themes for a "poetic child". The park-like fields and grassy meres each have their charms. Some of the meres surrounded by gloomy woods are still the reputed haunts of goblins who nightly wander here and hold unhallowed feasts.

A. D. Bayne, *The Illustrated History of Eastern England*

11. DRAAWN

I have very recently – February 1834 – seen the boy and his parents, who was *draawn* through my young ash at Woodbridge . . . I often see the boy. He is about eight years old. His mother has assured me that it was a sad case – "so painful, and so *tedious* was the child, that she got no rest night nor day" – and that the child – about six months old when *draawn* – immediately, or very soon, became composed, decidedly mended, and gradually recovered as the tree did; and has ever since remained well. His parents only were present at the operation. I have occasionally called to tell the mother of the well-doing of the tree – evidently to her satisfaction . . . I have little doubt but I could find out half a score of persons who have been *draawn* in their infancy, and cured, in and about Woodbridge. At my last visit to the cured boy, his father, at my request, furnished me with the following memorandum in his own writing: – "In putting a child through a tree first observe it must be early in the spring before the tree begin to vegitate 2ly the tree must be split as near east and west as it can 3ly it must be done just as the sun is rising 4ly the child must be stript quick naked 5 it must be put through the tree feet foremost 6 it must be turned round with the sun and observe it must be put through the tree three times and next you must be careful to close the tree in a proper manner and bind it up close with some new buss or something to answer as well – James Lord was put through and was cured, Mrs Shimming of Pittistree had 3 children born" (a word, perhaps *ruptured*, is omitted) "and Mr. Whitbread gave her a tree for each of them and was all cured and there is a man now living in Woodbridge who when a child was cured in the same way."

Edward Moor, *Oriental Fragments*

12. WEEDS

I have heard it confidently announced as if there could be no doubt about it, that weeds are natural to the ground, in the sense that the ground originates them; and that no man ever did, because no man ever could, eradicate them. They spring eternal from the ground itself, not at all necessarily from the seeds of parent weeds . . . To this ignorance is super-added in the case of weeds a theological conception, that the ground has been cursed with weeds as a punishment for man's disobedience. It has therefore ever borne, and will ever continue to bear, for the punishment of the husbandman (but why should husbandmen only be punished) thistles and poppies and speargrass.

F. Barham Zincke, *Some Materials for the History of Wherstead*

13. Suffolk Fair Maids

It seems the God of Nature hath been bountiful in giving them beautiful complexions, which I am willing to believe so far forth as it fixeth not a comparative disparagement on the same sex in other counties. I hope they will labour to join gracious hearts to fair faces; otherwise, I am sure, there is a divine proverb of infallible truth, "As a jewel of gold in a swine's snout, so is a fair woman which is without discretion."

Thomas Fuller, *The Worthies of England*

14. And Fair Providence

To conclude our description of Suffolk, I wish that therein grain of all kinds may be had at so reasonable rates, that rich and poor may be contented therewith. But if a famine should happen here, let the poor not distrust Divine Providence, whereof their grandfathers had so admirable a testimony, 1586, when, in a general dearth all over England, plenty of pease did grow on the sea-shore near Dunwich (never set or sown by human industry) which, being gathered in full ripeness, much abated the high prices in the markets, and preserved many hundreds of hungry families from famishing.

Thomas Fuller, *The Worthies of England*

15. Language

To come unto the persons themselves of this country inhabitants, when I remember their names and language, I find no dialect or idiom in the same different from others of the best speach and pronunciation ... Howbeit I must confesse our honest country toyling villager to expresse his meaning to his like neighbour, will many times lett slip some strang different sounding tearmes, no wayes intelligible to any of civill education, vntill by the rude comment of some skillfull in that forme, which by daily vse amongst them is familier, they bee after their manner explaned.

Richard Ryece, *The Breviary of Suffolk*

16. A Near One

Sudbourne was a rare poaching venue; they would go there in gangs. This was before the days when you could be had up for the job; you could be warned off but not prosecuted. Button said he had plenty o' them bits o' paper, enough to decorate a small room! On one occasion they went off there and were busy when they suddenly heard some tapping going on. Tap, tap, tap, it went; tap, tap, tap, until they found the noise was caused by a man tapping on a tree. Old Smoky White, a little lame "owd" chap, who spat or spluttered as he talked, came along and danced round the man by the tree, looking up into his face and exclaimed, "Sp . . . rt, sp . . . rt, whew are yeow? whew are yeow? Why, yare the Peep-o-Day man, arn't yew?" And they got on with the job. The man at the tree went on tapping and in between times cried in a faint voice, "I say, thare; wat are yew a dewin' on? I say, there!" Presently the keepers came on the scene, the company was rounded up and seen off down the village. As they were going along with the Tapper bringing up the rear, Button lagged behind and began to remonstrate with him.

"Yeouw hev done a fine thing; yew hev done my poor children out o' thare breakfast!"

"Well thare," said the Tapper, "I'm sorry tew hare about thet; hare's a shullun fur yew. Come agin as sune as yew kin, fur we git two-an'-six each extra fur seein' yew fellas off the estate!"

Egging-time provided Button with some of his greatest thrills. They would go about in parties and collect the eggs; then worth a shilling each. Rob one lot of gamekeepers and sell the eggs to another lot or even sell them back to those they had stolen them from. One morning they had gone Halesworth way, had a good haul, and Plummer was deputed to bring them home. It should be mentioned that the one found with the eggs was the one to go to prison. The eggs were carried inside their slops which had been fastened purse-like about their middle by a piece of string. Button came home by train, and as it drew into Darsham station his carriage stopped just in front of a policeman who was there seeing what could be seen.

"That's a rare nice marnin', George," was his amiable greeting.

"That that sartinly is," replied the quivering George as he made off as quick as ever he could; though why the policeman should have been looking for him was best known to his conscience. All the same he felt uncommonly warm. Over the fields he went to his home as fast as his "owd" legs would carry him; harnessed his horse and was off to Southwold to get rid of the uncomfortable cargo. As he was going up the Town Allen hill at Westleton, who should he espy coming out of his cottage and bundling into his tunic as fast as he could but the village policeman.

"Hi!" shouted he to Button, "I want yew. Hold hard a minute!"

Button, ever ready and vigilant, waved his arm frantically in reply and shouted, "Can't stop nohow! I'm in a tarin' hurry. I'll call as I come back." Besides, he had a nag that if so much as he had touched her flanks with his whip would have put a clean set of heels between him and danger. However, on the return he duly called.

"Ah, George," remarked the policeman, "that wur a near one!"

"Yis," agreed George, "but thet wornt near enough!"

Allan Jobson, *This Suffolk*

17. JOHN GAINSBOROUGH

There is an unfounded but wholly engaging local legend concerning 'The Bear' and Thomas Gainsborough's amazing brother John. John Gainsborough did not attain the international or even the national repute of his younger brother Tom, but he enjoyed considerable local fame. He was known to all Sudbury as "Scheming Jack", and at an early age he established for himself a reputation for eccentricity by his repeated attempts to build a flying machine. Destiny being what it is, and the first half of the 18th century not being a ripe time for the conquest of the air, "Scheming Jack" turned his hand to more reasonable inventions, among which were a self-rocking cradle and a mechanical cuckoo; the former enterprise is said to have been successful, and to have enjoyed great popularity among the weary mothers of Sudbury and district.

Now John also had some talent for painting, and this brings us to his alleged connection with 'The Bear'. The landlord – so the story goes – commissioned "Scheming Jack" to paint a signboard. The fee offered was twenty shillings. "Make it thirty," John is reputed to have said, "and I will tie your bear up with a nice gold chain." But a sovereign was the landlord's price, and so the bear was duly painted – minus his chain. The next morning he found a laughing crowd gathered in the roadway before the Inn, and everyone was looking up at the new signboard. Wondering, the landlord came out to investigate the cause of all the merriment. He soon knew. The bear had completely disappeared from the picture. The background was intact, and where a bear had been superimposed on it there was now an empty silhouette. "Ah!" sighed Jack sympathetically when the landlord remonstrated with him. "You should have let me tie him up!" The bear had been sketched in with soluble distemper and the previous night there had been rain!

Leonard P. Thompson, *Old Inns of Suffolk*

18. WEDDINGS AND PROSPECTS

When we first came here wives were still kept in subjection just as they had been before the 'votes for women' agitation; wife-beating was still practised, the husband in question taking care to abide by the alleged legal requirement and to use a stick not thicker than a man's thumb;

also that detestable custom of the eighteenth century, referred to in Smollett's *Humphrey Clinker* which Suffolk calls a 'rough wedding.' When the newly married couple retires to bed a gang of young men gather round outside the cottage, with tin pans and anything that will make a noise and start banging the pans and hallooing; the wretched bridegroom has to rise and come downstairs and give them all a drink before they will go away. I have not heard of a similar case for over twenty years and I trust the custom is dead. Nowadays, all farmworkers go away for a honeymoon; perhaps the fear of a rough wedding was originally one of the motives for this.

The old doctor, Dr. Wilkin, told me that fifty years ago about a third of the births were illegitimate; the position is now very different, but the doctor attributed this to increased knowledge, rather than a higher standard of morality. The birth of an illegitimate child seems to have no effect on the future marriage prospects of the girl, and it is a common thing for the eldest child of a family to be markedly different from the rest of the children.

One of the Suffolk stories is this. A young man was going out with a girl, when his father drew him aside and said: "You mustn't court that girl – she's my daughter." The next girl he courted, the same result occurred; but when it happened a third time, he went off to his mother in a fury and said to her: "You didn't ought to have let Father carry on so," – to which she replied: "Don't you take no heed of what he say, he ain't your father."

Justin and Edith Brooke, Suffolk Prospect

19. SILLY SUFFOLK

"A fine horse! a capital horse!" said several of the connoisseurs. "What do you ask for him?" "Too much for any of you to pay," said I. "A horse like this is intended for other kind of customers than any of you." "How do you know that?" said one; the very same person whom I had heard complaining in the street of the paucity of good horses in the fair. "Come, let us know what you ask for him?" "A hundred and fifty pounds!" said I; "neither more nor less." "Do you call that a great price?" said the man. "Why I thought you would have asked double that amount! You do yourself injustice, young man." "Perhaps I do," said I, "but that's my affair; I do not choose to take more." "I wish you would let me get into the saddle," said the man; "the horse knows you, and therefore shows to more advantage; but I should like to see how he would move under me, who am a stranger. Will you let me get into the saddle, young man?" "No," said I; "I will not let you get into the saddle." "Why not?" said the man. "Lest you should be a Yorkshireman," said I; "and should run away with the horse." "Yorkshire?" said the man; "I am from Suffolk – silly Suffolk – so you need not be afraid of my running away with the horse." "Oh! if that's the case," said I, "I should be afraid that the horse would run away with you; so I will by no means let you mount." "Will you let me look in his mouth?" said the man. "If you please," said I; "but I tell you, he's apt to bite." "He can scarcely be a worse bite than his master," said the man, looking into the horse's mouth; "he's four off. I say, young man, will you warrant this horse" "No," said I; "I never warrant horses; the horses that I ride can always warrant themselves."

George Borrow, *The Romany Rye*

Some Suffolk Celebrations

20. FAIRINGS

Thomas: *By my troth, Margaret, here's a weather is able to make a man*
           call his father "whoreson": if this weather hold, we shall have hay
           good cheap, and butter and cheese at Harleston will bear no price.

Margaret: *Thomas, maids when they come to see the fair*
           Count not to make a cope for dearth of hay:
           When we have turn'd our butter to the salt,
           And set our cheese safely upon the racks,
           Then let our fathers prize it as they please.
           We country sluts of merry Fressingfield
           Come to buy needless naughts to make us fine,
           And look that young men should be frank this day,
           And court us with such fairings as they can.
           Phoebus is blithe, and frolic looks from heaven,
           As when he courted lovely Semele,
           Swearing the pedlers shall have empty packs,
           If that fair weather may make chapmen buy.

Lacy: *But, lovely Peggy, Semele is dead,*
           And therefore Phoebus from his palace pries,
           And, seeing such a sweet and seemly saint,
           Shows all his glories for to court yourself.

Margaret: *This is a fairing, gentle sir, indeed,*
           To soothe me up with such sweet flattery;
           But learn of me, your scoff's too broad before.—
           Well, Joan, our beauties must abide their jests;
           We serve the turn in jolly Fressingfield.

Joan: *Margaret,*
           A farmer's daughter for a farmer's son;
           I warrant you, the meanest of us both
           Shall have a mate to lead us from the church

(Lacy whispers Margaret in the ear)
But, Thomas, what's the news? what, in a dump?
Give me your hand, we are near a pedler's shop;
Out with your purse, we must have fairings now.
Thomas: *Faith, Joan, and shall: I'll bestow a fairing on you, and then we*
will to the tavern, and snap off a pint of wine or two.
Margaret: *Whence are you, sir? of Suffolk? for your terms*
Are finer than the common sort of men.
Lacy: *Faith, lovely girl, I am of Beccles by,*
Your neighbour, not above six miles from hence,
A farmer's son that never was so quaint
But that he could do courtesy to such dames.

Robert Greene, *Friar Bacon and Friar Bungay*

21. OUR MIDSUMMER HOLIDAYS

When the Bedingfields reached the ground on which the sports were to be held, a noble sight presented itself. Broadmeadow, which was an area of more than twenty acres, was surrounded on every side with company. Wagons and carts, and tumbrils and phaeton-carriages, and donkey-chaises, and every other species of vehicle, exclusive of sledges, were packed neatly around the field, leaving a broad open space, in the centre of which arose an immense straight stick or pole, fifty feet high, with a leg of mutton, garnished with red ribbons, on the top of it. It was very pleasing to observe with what interest the rustics looked upon that leg of mutton. Tears came into the eyes – no, the *mouths* – of many who looked at it: with visions of a glorious Sunday dinner, when the exalted viand should have left its proud position at the "head of the pole", and settled itself over a large dish of baked potatoes, he himself being done brown in his cuisine translation. The ribbons floated in the breeze, the sounds of rustic music broke upon the ear, a clarionet, a tambourine, and a triangle, kept up a kind of clamour, till at last the band of the Wilford Volunteers came on in gorgeous military array, playing appropriately, "Oh! the Roast Beef of Old England! Oh! the old English Roast Beef!" And well might they play it, for at the upper end of the broad meadow was a large marquee, where roast beef (cold, of course) displayed itself in all the glorious qualities of fat and lean for which it is so famous, while around it, as supporters of the great national emblem, like threatening cannon-balls on every side, were ranged plum puddings without stint; and there were great hams also, and other more delicate viands for the gentry, such as ducks, capons, tongues, and other trifles, the whole being garnished with flowers, and green ears of wheat, barley, oats and the like, giving an agricultural character to the whole.

In the midst of the hubbub which followed the cessation of the martial music of the band, was seen old Sir Hubert himself on a fine old hunter, his wife riding by his side on a handsome palfrey, and his daughter on a roan cob, and two little grandsons on Shetlands. The appearance of the knight was the signal for a shout which rent the welkin, if you know what that is. His cavalcade rode down the middle and up the sides of the assembled throng, while cheer after cheer followed it. The knight took up his position in front of the greased pole, and, after sundry flourishes of trumpet and drum, the sports began.

'Peter Parsley', Our Midsummer Holidays, from *Peter Parsley's Annual*

22. AFTER HARVEST

Figure to yourself, reader, a long well-wooded lane or natural avenue, leading from field to field or meadow to meadow; in spring time its banks redolent of white and purple violets, in summer, its hedges a tangle of wild rose and honeysuckle, overhead stately oak and elm lending perpetual shadow, musical with wood pigeon and little birds. Except for occasional passage of lazy herd or tumbril slowly making way over grass green ruts, all is quiet and solitary. The drift indeed belongs to the farm, as much as orchard or potato garden. A delicious retreat when no young colts are disporting themselves in its precincts is the pightle, now a glory of cowslips, sweetest of all sweet flowers, now of wild clover, pasturage of the bees. A breeze blows freshly even in July, there are no sultry days in my beloved Suffolk, and here also the idler would find himself alone . . .

That bygone pastoral, I am tempted to say pageant, has never been supplanted by richer, more varied experiences. With the reaping machine, the patent mower, the steam thresher vanished all poetry from cornfield and farmyard. With the improved kitchener, mechanical churner, and the inroads of generality, farmhouse life has become prosaic as that of a stocking factory. But in former days it was not so. Hardship there might be, boorishness there might be, yet a bucolic spirit from time to time reigned in these homely scenes, for a brief interval existence wore the aspect of Bacchanalia. Their ruddy faces gleaming like red hot coals against the golden sheaves, the lusty reapers obeyed beck and nod of the "Lord of the Harvest", leader chosen for his prowess, commanding presence and high character generally. At a signal from the lord all filed off to the nearest hedge for "bait" and "bever" i.e. eleven and four o'clock collations of harvest cake and beer, a can of the oldest and strongest being supplied from the farm upon extra occasions. Decency characterised the conversation, oft-times master and men sitting down to bait and bever together.

Meantime at home housewives were busy. Alike in farm and cottage huge plumpuddings would dance in the boiler, before the dinner-hour being taken up to cool. What a commotion among the wasps! No matter the devices resorted to, as well try to keep schoolboys from green apples as drive away wasps from a harvest pudding. To this day the sight of a wasp recalls that savoury steam on the window sill.

But the crowing gala was the coming home of the last waggon. When both crops and weather had proved propitious, when farmer and reapers were in high spirits, and, above all, when the moon was full, this was a festival indeed.

Long before the procession approached joyous shouts and singing announced the culminating event of the husbandman's year, the prosperous gathering in, the happy close of so many anxious nights and laborious days. Louder and louder grows the chorus of untrained voices, more distinct the tramp of feet and rumble of wheels; then in the summer twilight, the harvest moon rising in full splendour behind it, appears the last waggon today, a triumphal car decorated with green boughs and field flowers.

M. Betham Edwards, *Reminiscences*

23. Harvest Home

Behold the sound oak table's massy frame
Bestride the kitchen floor! the careful dame,
And gen'rous host invite their friends around,
For all that clear'd the crop, or till'd the ground,
Are guests by right of custom:– old and young;
And many a neighbouring yeoman join the throng,
With artizans that lent their dext'rous aid,
When o'er each field the flaming sun-beams play'd.

Yet Plenty reigns, and from her boundless hoard,
Though not one jelly trembles on the board,
Supplies the feast with all that sense can crave;
With all that made our great forefathers brave,
Ere the cloy'd palate countless flavours try'd,
And cooks had Nature's judgment set aside.
With thanks to Heaven, and tales of rustic lore,
The mansion echoes when the banquet's o'er;
A wider circle spreads, and smiles abound,
As quick the frothing horn performs its round;
Care's mortal foe; that sprightly joys imparts
To cheer the frame and renovate their hearts.
Here, fresh and brown, the hazel's produce lies

In tempting heaps, and peals of laughter rise,
And crackling Music, with the frequent Song,
Unheeded bear the midnight hour along.

Here once a year Distinction low'rs its crest,
The master, servant, and the merry guest,
Are equal all; and round the happy ring
The reaper's eyes exulting glances fling,
And, warm'd with gratitude, he quits his place,
With sun-burnt hands and ale-enliven'd face,
Refills the jug his honour'd host to tend,
To serve at once the master and the friend;
Proud thus to meet his smiles, to share his tale,
His nuts, his conversation, and his ale.

Robert Bloomfield, *The Farmer's Boy*

24. A More Prosaic View

Kessingland, a village amid fields, looks pretty with its church-tower backed by trees. A labourer who had, as he said, been "spreeding muck", and was sitting down to rest "afoor goin' back to Kess'land", took the opportunity to ease his mind on what was to him a grievance: the disuse of old harvest customs. "Why!" he said, in the sing-song tone of the Suffolk rustic, "I remembers when there used to be three frollucks (frolics) at harvest-time: one afoor they begun, one in the middle, and one when they'd done. Then the farmers got down to two frollucks; then they got down to one; then they took to givin' half a crown and none, and at last nawthin'. And now if ye do but look at the pump they axes ye what ye want, as if a drop o' water was too much for a baw. Dash 'em! I say, why can't they let us hev our largesse again as we used to hev it? What's ten shillin' a-week?"

The old story. Here was one who would have liked a revival of the "Horkey" such as Bloomfield describes,

When up they got full drive, and then
Went out to halloo largess"

and when there was a lord over the reapers, and the merry-making, in which, as the poet sings, it was

— found out they talk'd the louder, the oft'ner pass'd the horn"

It was an old custom, for Tusser mentions it while recommending that reaping should be day work:

> *"Grant harvest-lord, by a penny or two,*
> *To call on his fellows the better to do:*
> *Give gloves to thy reapers, a largess to cry*
> *And daily to loiterers have a good eye."*

There is a jocund sound about it that seems to accord with a great rural festival; but the gladness always degenerated into uproar and drunkenness; and any right-minded person who remembers what Suffolk peasants were thirty years ago, will hold that "nawthin'" is better than the old coarse "frollucks". I told the labourer he might as well ask for restoration of Covehithe and Easton Bavent as for revival of the Horkey, and suggested that the improved harvest-homes which some intelligent and kindhearted proprietors had recently set on foot were worth consideration. "I dun knaw", was all he answered.

Walter White, Eastern England

25. HARVEST

> *The Suffolk skies are pale and bright*
> *Its ocean airs are keen,*
> *Dark and jolly*
> *Is hedgerow holly*
> *With white stems in between,*
> *A peasant woman, homely dight*
> *Gleans slowly in the pure twilight*
> *Where harvesters have been.*

Sir Francis Newbolt, The Enchanted Wood

26. A SUFFOLK GAME – CAMP

A game formerly much in use among schoolboys, and occasionally played by men in those parts of Suffolk on the sea coast – more especially in the line of Hollesley Bay between the Rivers Orwell and Alde – sometimes school against school or parish against parish. It was thus played –

Goals were pitched at the distance of 150 or 200 yards from each other – these were generally formed of the thrown off clothes of the competitors. Each party has two goals, ten or fifteen yards apart. The parties, ten or fifteen on a side, stand in line, facing their own goals and each other, at about ten yards distance, midway between the goals, and nearest that of their adversaries. An indifferent spectator, agreed on by the parties, throws up a ball, of the size of a common cricket ball, midway between the confronted players, and makes his escape. It is the object of the players to seize and convey the ball between their own goals. The rush is therefore very great; as is sometimes the shock of the first onset, to catch the falling ball:– he who first can catch or seize it speeds therefore home pursued by his opponents (thro' whom he has to make his way) aided by the jostlings and various assistances of his own *sidesmen*. If caught and held, or in imminent danger of being caught, he *throws* the ball – but must in no case *give* it – to a less beleaguered friend, who, if it be not arrested in its course or he jostled away by the eager and watchful adversaries, catches it; and he hastens homeward, in like manner pursued, annoyed, and aided – winning the notch (or snotch) if he contrive to *carry* – not *throw* – it between his goals. But this in a well matched game, is no easy achievement, and often requires much time, many doublings, detours and exertions. I should have noticed that if the holder of the ball be caught with the ball in his possession, he loses a *snotch*, if, therefore, he be hard pressed, he throws it to a convenient friend, more free and in breath than himself. At the loss (or gain) of a *snotch*, a recommence takes place, arranging which gives the parties time to take breath. Seven or nine notches are the game – and these it will sometimes take two or three hours to win.

It is a most noble and manly sport; in the whole little, if at all, inferior to cricket, or hunting, or horse-racing . . . The sport and name are very old. The "Camping pightel" occurs in a deed of the 30 Hen. 6 – about 1486. Cullum's Hawstead, p. 113 where Tusser is quoted in proof, that not only was the exercise manly and salutary, but good also for the *pightel* or meadow.

> *In meadow or pasture – (to grow the more fine)*
> *Let campers be camping in any of thine:*
> *Which if ye do suffer when low is the spring,*
> *You gain to yourself a commodious thing* (p. 65)

And he says in page 56,

> *Get campers a ball*
> *To camp therewithall.*

Ray says that the game prevails in Norfolk, Suffolk and Essex; and he derives it from the Saxon *Camp*, to strive. The Latin *Campus*, a field, or, according to Ainsworth, a *plain field*, may have its share in the name.

Since this was written a friend informs me that this game fell into disuse in Suffolk, in consequence of two men having been killed at Easton about forty or fifty years ago, in their struggles at a grand match.

Edward Moor, *Suffolk Words and Phrases*

27. A Fighting Camp

In the middle of the eighteenth century there was a great match between Norfolk and Suffolk on Diss Common, each team consisting of 300 man. Apparently the Norfolk men were very sure of victory, for when they came upon the field they tauntingly asked the Suffolk men whether they had brought their coffins with them, but after fourteen hours play! had transformed the ground into a battlefield, the Suffolk team were declared the victors. Such games were called "fighting camps" and it is not surprising that nine deaths resulted from the one in question within a fortnight, nor is it strange that such encounters eventually fell into disfavour.

W. A. Dutt, *Highways and Byeways of East Anglia*

28. Ceremonies

The evening before the wheat harvest begins the men 'wet the sickle', i.e. take an allowance of beer. This beer is often drunk at the public house, and is the amount given by the farmer as 'earnest' when hired for the harvest (generally 1s. a man) and as much more as they like to spend.

A custom exists among harvestmen in some parts of Suffolk called 'ten pounding'. In most reaps there is a set of rules agreed on by the reapers before harvest, by which they are governed during its continuance. The object of these rules is usually to prevent or punish loss of time by laziness, drunkenness, etc.; and to correct swearing, lying, or quarrelling among themselves; or any other kind of misbehaviour which might slacken the exertions or break the harmony of the reap.

One of the modes of punishment directed by these rules is called 'ten pounding' and is executed in the following manner. Upon the breach of any of the rules a sort of drum-head court martial is held upon the delinquent, and, if he is found guilty, he is instantly seized and thrown flat on his back; some of the party keep his head down and confine his arms, whilst others turn his legs up so as to exhibit his posterior. The person who is to inflict the punishment then takes a shoe and with the heel of it (studded as it usually is with hob-nails) gives him the prescribed number of blows according to the sentence. The rest of the party sit by, with their hats off, to see that the executioner does his duty, and if he fails in this he undergoes the same punishment . . .

Hallooing largess. We apply the word 'largess' (which was anciently in extensive use by heralds and others) to a gift in harvest time – usually of a shilling – to the reapers, who ask and expect it of visitors to the harvest field. For this the reapers assemble in a ring, holding each others' hands and inclining their heads to the centre; one of the party, detached a few yards, calls loudly thrice, "Holla lar, Holla lar, Holla lar-g-e-e-ss", lowering the voice at the last lengthened syllable. Those in the ring lengthen out o-o- with a low sonorous note and inclined heads, and then throwing their heads up vociferate a-a-ah . . .

A man receiving a shilling will ask you if you choose to have it hallooed. If answered in the affirmative he collects his fellow workmen, and they halloo it forthwith, otherwise they halloo the whole day's receipts towards the close of the evening.

The Horkey. The last or 'horkey' load is decorated with flags and streamers. This load is attended by all reapers etc. with hallooing and shouting. On their arrival at the farmyard the mistress and maids come out to gladden their eyes with the welcome scene and bestir themselves to prepare the substantial and homely feast . . .

A rustic drama is usually acted on these occasions, which greatly increases the merriment; one of the revellers, habited as a female, feigns to be taken with a violent toothache, and the 'doctor' is sent for. He soon appears mounted on the back of one of the other men (the 'horse' has a milking stool to bear his hands upon to keep his back level); the 'doctor' brings with him the tongs which he uses for the purpose of extracting the tooth; this is a piece of tobacco pipe placed in the mouth; a fainting takes place from the violence of the operation, and the bellows are employed as a means of restoring the pretended sufferer . . .

W. and H. Raynbird, On the Agriculture of Suffolk

VII. A DIGRESSION ON CHEESE

Most counties seem to have one curiosity on which successive generations of commentators remark: in Suffolk's case, it would appear to be cheese which has always attracted comment. The following is only a brief selection:—

1.　　　　*Unrivall'd stands thy country cheese, O Giles;*
　　　　Whose very name alone engenders smiles;
　　　　Whose fame abroad by every tongue is spoke,
　　　　The well-known butt of many a flinty joke,
　　　　That pass like current coin the nation through;
　　　　And, ah! experience proves the satire true.

Robert Bloomfield, *The Farmer's Boy*

2. The Suffolk butter is much esteemed; but alas! those, who make good butter, must, of course, make bad cheese; and therefore the generality of Suffolk cheese is well known to be as remarkably bad, as the butter is excellent. But in those districts where little or no butter is churned, as good cheese is made as any in the kingdom, being little, if at all, inferior to that of Stilton . . .

Hunger will break through stone walls, or any thing, except Suffolk cheese, says Ray. Suffolk cheese, from its poverty, says Grose, is frequently the subject of much humour. It is by some represented as only fit for making wheels for wheelbarrows; and a story is told, that a parcel of Suffolk cheese being packed up in an iron chest, and put on board a ship bound to the East Indies, the rats, allured by the scent, eat through the chest, but could not penetrate the cheese.

James Ford (Ed.), *The Suffolk Garland*

3. If I should here sett downe what great profitt doth arise from these dairies, both for butter and cheese, or if I should speake of the great commendation which by our histories at home, and by writers abroad, in former times have been given to the goodnesse and excellency of this cheese, by which they never doubted to compare it with any other cheese of any forraine nation whatsoever. I might peradventure speake beyond common creditt . . . All of which I speake to this end, whilst in the dayes of our forefathers this shire carried away the prize for excellency of this kind, at this day it is suspected, and the wonted estimation much abated; for whilst every one striving to make the most of their dairy, holding outt

in the wonted proportion, butt much giving in in the wonted quality, it cannot bee that things should be so currant as they were wont to bee in times past.

Richard Ryece, *The Breviary of Suffolk*

4. This part is generally very dirty and fruitful. In this part is made the Suffolk butter, so managed by the neat dairy-wife, that it is justly esteemed the pleasantest and best in England. The cheese, if right made, none much better, and if not so, none can be worse.

John Kirby, *The Suffolk Traveller*

5. But those few in these parts who make little or no butter, make as good cheese, as any in Warwickshire, Gloucestershire, or any other parts of the kingdom; insomuch, that it sells for tenpence and twelvepence a pound, or more; being little, if at all, inferior to that of Stilton.

Ibid (Second Edition)

6. Cheese. Most excellent are made herein, whereof the finest are very thin, as intended not for food but digestion. I remember, when living in Cambridge, the cheese of this county was preferred as the best. If any say that scholars' palates are incompetent judges, whose hungry appetites make coarse diet seem delicates unto them, let them know that Pantaleon, the learned Dutch physician, counted them equal at least with them of Parma in Italy.

Thomas Fuller, *The Worthies of England*

7. Suffolk cheese is proverbially execrable . . . It must be presumed that the art of cheese-making has considerably declined in Suffolk since Fuller's days . . .

Rev. Alfred Suckling, *History of Antiquities of the County of Suffolk*

8. I was not so enthusiastic about the local made cheese, although always a lover of this edible. It bore the name of "Suffolk Bang" at that time. Why, I do not know, unless in its solidity it was recognised as a good substitute for cannon balls. Now, however, it is quite a different story.

The teaching of the true art of dairy work in the Eastern counties since my young time has produced a cheese quite equal to the finest Cheddar. There is one kind of cheese, however, to which the foregoing remarks could not be held to apply, namely the home-made "Suffolk Cream Cheese" which always was and still is, unbeatable. Should any of my readers find themselves on a Saturday in Ipswich be sure to visit the Provision Market, held in the Corn Exchange building, and procure a sample of this celebrated delicacy. It is not by any means dear.

O. R. Wellbanks, Suffolk, My County

VIII. A PERSONAL SELECTION

This final selection contains a miscellany of writings which seem to me, in their different ways, to illuminate aspects of Suffolk which constitute its appeal. This is the "personal" selection to which I have already referred: without any desire or intention to root the lines by Henry Howard in a particular landscape, I can only observe that to me they speak of Suffolk. For the rest, Julian Tennyson's wonderful book "Suffolk Scene" almost defies the anthologer's scissors – I have taken a passage from it which shows him at his most personal. Edward Fitzgerald – and Tennyson's greeting to him – go together, and have to be in, as do lines by Suffolk's greatest poet, Crabbe. The final two bits of prose speak for themselves, the extract from "Joseph and his Brethren" coming as close as anything I know to the authentic Suffolk voice. If there is any theme to this last section, it is that there is no idyllic Suffolk; its beauty is tinged with melancholy and its strongest urge is the unceasing, hard-fought human round.

1. SUMMER

> The soote Season that bud and bloom forth brings
> With green hath clad the hill and eke the vale:
> The Nightingall with fethers new she sings:
> The Turtle to her mate hath told her tale.
> Summer is come: for every spray now springs.
> The Hart hath hung his old head on the pale;
> The Buck in brake his winter coat he flings;
> The Fishes fleete with new repayred scale:
> The Adder all her slough away she flings;
> The swift Swallow pursueth the flies smalle.
> The busy Bee her honey how she minges!
> Winter is worne that was the floures bale.
> And thus I see among these pleasant things
> Eche care decays; and yet my sorrow springs.

Henry Howard, Earl of Surrey

2. DAWN IN SUFFOLK

Anyone who has ever got out of bed at the best time of the day knows what an ordinary dawn looks like, a dawn over woods, field or town; but the ardent wildfowler sees a dawn of unique and unbelievable loveliness.

Those who have never been abroad in summer on a marsh or river during the hour before sunrise have missed the most wonderful moments of a lifetime.

In the first darkness you can distinguish nothing, nothing save the pale band of the river and the jagged masses of the distant woods, like broken and blackened teeth in the jaw of an old giant. The silence is cool and hostile, enveloping your whole mind and body and reducing you to a small, shivering unit in the universal subjection of its influence. There is no life anywhere; not a bird calls, not a reed stirs, there is not even breath or colour in the earth itself.

By and by a long green strip, very luminous and hard, edges the deep blackness on the eastern horizon. It broadens; the stars give ground a little; a pale, transparent film spreads slowly up the sky, like a faint and phosphorescent gauze laid over a black cloth. For a while the silence lies more chilly than ever. And then from those dark, dented woods comes the sudden and lusty crow of an old cock pheasant, breaking upon the world like the ringing of an alarm-bell in a sleeping town. It is a signal. At once there bursts forth the most wonderful and tremendous clamour ever heard in Suffolk's quiet countryside. In front of you the triumphant crow of pheasants, the urgent caw of rooks, the gently plaint of woodpigeons, the staccato jukking of partridges; behind you the scream of gulls, the nervous chatter of dunlin, the shrill pipe of redshank, the querulous wail of curlew and whimbrel, the throaty cackle of mallard and shelduck, the hoarse bark of ill-tempered old herons; all these and a score of other voices are mingled together in mighty concert, and the whole air throbs with the beauty and amazement of it. It is a noise fantastic, bewildering and glorious. Perhaps for three or four minutes it is above you, around you, within you, sweeping you away on its mad cacophony; and then, as suddenly as it arose, it dies again, dies on a single note, like a crescendo broken off at the fall of the conductor's baton. And at once the very silence stuns you.

But the silence does not last for long. The birds of marsh and field and wood and river are on the move once more, and the veil is quickly lifting on another day. That green film across the sky, forgotten during the chorus of the birds, is growing stronger and stronger; it is surprising with what speed the light comes, and even more surprising how long is the interval between the coming of the light and the appearance of the sun himself. Now the marsh is piecing itself together; now you can distinguish landmarks, a stile, a derelict farm, a field of corn stooked on the previous day; now you can pick out the foremost trees from what a short while ago was nothing but a black, solid ridge of rock. And now, too, there moves before you the strangest phenomenon in all this miracle of dawn – the mist.

It seems to come suddenly out of the wood two miles away, a white, woolly phalanx mustering at the foot of the hill. For a moment it hangs uncertainly, shifting, wavering, and then it rolls readily forward, creeping breast-high over the dull plain of the marsh, like a cloud of dust before a line of horsemen. But as it nears you it is no longer a solid cloud; it is more like the vapour from a thousand small cauldrons in the earth, fragile and thin, slight and diaphanous, wreathing and curling into curious, restless shapes. The fingers of it stretch out to the bank, almost to your feet, clutching gently and helplessly at the heads of the reeds. And thus the mist stays, spread over the marsh, never rising, never settling, and the writhing strands grow fainter and thinner until at last they dissolve altogether.

All this while the light increases. The marsh is quite clear, though the colours of it are dull and lifeless. From every reed-head hangs a gossamer, sometimes three or four on a single stem, all of different shapes and sizes, all perfect and complete, all sparkling and swaying together. They were there in the darkness, and they will be there until the sun leaps up over the wood. Then for a moment they will glint and flash like opals turned under a strong light; at the climax of that moment they will wither and disappear, and with them will go the last vestige of night and of dawn. Once the sun is up there will be nothing further to keep you on the bank. The flight will be over. You will look all round the sky and see that not a duck is moving anywhere, and then you will know that it is time for you to make your way down the creek again.

Julian Tennyson, *Suffolk Scene*

2. OLD SONG

Tis a dull sight
To see the year dying,
When winter winds
Set the yellow wood sighing:
Sighing, O sighing!

When such a time cometh
I do retire
Into an old room
Beside a bright fire:
O, pile a bright fire!

And there I sit
Reading old things
Of knights and lorn damsels,
While the wind sings –
O, drearily sings!

I never look out
Nor attend to the blast;
For all to be seen
Is the leaves falling fast:
Falling, falling!

But close at the hearth
Like a cricket, sit I,
Reading of summer
And chivalry –
Gallant chivalry!

Then with an old friend
I talk of our youth –
How 'twas gladsome, but often
Foolish, forsooth:
But gladsome, gladsome!

Or, to get merry,
We sing some old rhyme
That made the wood ring again
In summer time –
Sweet summer time!

Then we go smoking,
Silent and snug:
Naught passes between us,
Save a brown jug –
Sometimes!

And sometimes a tear
Will rise in each eye,
Seeing the two old friends
So merrily –
So merrily!

And ere to bed
Go we, go we,
Down on the ashes
We kneel on the knee,
Praying together!

Thus, then, live I
Till, 'mid all the gloom,

By heaven! the bold sun
Is with me in the room
Shining, shining!

Then the clouds part,
Swallows soaring between;
The spring is alive,
And the meadows are green!

I jump up like mad,
Break the old pipe in twain,
And away to the meadows,
The meadows again!

Edward Fitzgerald

4. To E. Fitzgerald

OLD FITZ, who from your suburb grange,
Where once I tarried for a while,
Glance at the wheeling Orb of change,
And greet it with a kindly smile;
Whom yet I see as there you sit
Beneath your sheltering garden-tree,
And while your doves about you flit,
And plant on shoulder, hand and knee,
Or on your head their rosy feet,
As if they knew your diet spares
Whatever moved in that full sheet
Let down to Peter at his prayers;
Who live on milk and meal and grass;
And once for ten long weeks I tried
Your table of Pythagoras,
And seem'd at first 'a thing enskied'
(As Shakespeare has it) airy-light
To float above the ways of men,
Then fell from that half-spiritual height
Chill'd, till I tasted flesh again
One night when earth was winter-black,
And all the heavens flash'd in frost;
And on me, half asleep, came back
That wholesome heat the blood had lost,
And set me climbing icy capes
And glaciers, over which there roll'd

To meet me long-arm'd vines with grapes
Of Eshcol hugeness; for the cold
Without, and warmth within me, wrought
To mould the dream; but none can say
That Lenten fare makes Lenten thought,
Who reads your golden Eastern lay,
Than which I know no version done
In England more divinely well;
A planet equal to the sun
Which cast it, that large infidel
Your Omar; and your Omar drew
Full-handed plaudits from our best
In modern letters, and from two,
Old friends outvaluing all the rest,
Two voices heard on earth no more;
But we old friends are still alive,
And I am nearing seventy-four,
While you have touch'd at seventy-five,
And so I send a birthday line
Of greeting; and my son, who dipt
In some forgotten book of mine
With sallow scraps of manuscript,
And dating many a year ago,
Has hit on this, which you will take
My Fitz, and welcome, as I know
Less for its own than for the sake
Of one recalling gracious times,
When, in our younger London days,
You found some merit in my rhymes,
And I more pleasure in your praise.

Alfred, Lord Tennyson

5. OLD AGE

Ye gentle souls who dream of rural ease,
Whom the smooth stream and smoother sonnet please;
Go! if the peaceful cot your praises share,
Go look within, and ask if peace be there:
If peace be his – that drooping weary sire,
Or their's, that offspring round their feeble fire,
Or her's, that matron pale, whose trembling hand
Turns on the wretched hearth th'expiring brand.
Nor yet can time itself obtain for these
Life's latest comforts, due respect and ease;

For yonder see that hoary swain, whose age
Can with no cares except its own engage;
Who, propt on that rude staff, looks up to see
The bare arms broken from the withering tree;
On which a boy, he climb'd the loftiest bough,
Then his first joy, but his sad emblem now.

He once was chief in all the rustic trade,
His steady hand the straighest furrow made;
Full many a prize he won, and still is proud
To find the triumphs of his youth allow'd;

A transient pleasure sparkles in his eyes,
He hears and smiles, then thinks again and sighs;
For now he journeys to his grave in pain;
The rich disdain him; nay, the poor disdain;
Alternate masters now their slave command,
And urge the efforts of his feeble hand;
Who, when his age attempts its task in vain,
With ruthless taunts of lazy poor complain.

Oft may you see him when he tends the sheep,
His winter charge, beneath the hillock weep;
Oft hear him murmur to the winds that blow
O'er his white locks, and bury them in snow;
When rouz'd by rage and muttering in the morn,
He mends the broken hedge with icy thorn.
"Why do I live, when I desire to be
At once from life and life's long labour free?
Like leaves in spring, the young are blown away,
Without the sorrows of a slow decay;
I, like yon wither'd leaf, remain behind,
Nipt by the frost and shivering in the wind;
There it abides till younger buds come on,
As I, now all my fellow swains are gone;
Then, from the rising generation thrust,
It falls, like me, unnotic'd to the dust . . .

George Crabbe, *The Village*

6. Away From It All

Two of five brothers, from an East Suffolk farm, have determined to get away from the hopelessness of their life: and being sent to Ipswich by their harsh father, set about leaving Suffolk.

Ten minutes later found them in the booking-hall of the station.

"Do you ask, Bob, this time", said Hiram. "I did it last time."

"No, do you do it", said Bob. "You'd put it better'n I should."

"All right", said Hiram, poking his head through the trap door of the booking-office. "Can you tell me how to get to Canada, mister?"

The booking-clerk looked rather puzzled for a moment; then, his practical sense asserting itself, he frowned and said:

"You'll have to go to Liverpool first to get a boat."

Hiram turned to Bob.

"We've got to go to Liverpool first", he repeated.

"Well", answered Bob, "let's go to Liverpool, Hiram."

"How do you get to Liverpool, mister?" said Hiram, turning to the booking-clerk again.

"Take the next train to Peterborough and change", he replied irritably.

"Well, let's have two tickets to Liverpool, mister", said Hiram. "Two single third class."

The clerk slapped two tickets down in front of him.

"It do fare an awful lot of money, mister", said Hiram, carefully untying the string of the little leather bag that held his savings and taking out some sovereigns.

"Do you want the tickets or don't you?" snapped the clerk. "You don't expect to get there for nothing, do you?"

"All right, mister", said Hiram apologetically. "Here you are."

Half an hour later they were seated in opposite corners of a railway carriage, jogging slowly towards Peterborough through the placid landscapes of West Suffolk and staring out of the window with all the interest of schoolboys on holiday, and to men like them, unused to travelling, a train journey was as good as a holiday. But they could not long forget what was for them the principal business of life as farm after farm unfolded itself before them: a farmer is perennially curious of the way other people farm.

"There's a rum 'un for you", cried Bob excitedly, pointing to a piece of ploughland at the side of the line. "The chap as did that was a jim and no mistake. Look at his hidland: he couldn't plough straight even when he had the hedge to go by."

"No, that he couldn't", said Hiram. "That's a nice piece of winter wheat over there: that look well."

"Not so well as ours though", said Bob proudly. "My! Hiram, there's lambs for you. Did you ever see such poor little owd things?"

"He don't know how to feed 'em, he don't", said Hiram, shaking his head ruefully. "He's a bad farmer. Look at the rubbish in that field there; his turnips 'on't live long. Nice beans those."

"Almost as good as ourn", replied Bob grudgingly. "But come to think of it, Hiram, hev you seen any land that look as forrard and well-kept as ourn?"

"No", said Hiram reflectively, "I hev not; and what's more, I've not seen no horses that look as if they had a real good bait every morning like we give ours: and you can tell by the way their coats look. And the cows too and the lambs. Fare to me they don't know how to feed their beasts in these parts."

"No", said Bob in a more subdued voice, "Crakenhill is a tidy little farm and no mistake."

They both abruptly stopped talking and the silence was not broken until after they had left Bury St. Edmunds behind them. The train was unusually empty and they still had the carriage to themselves, which was important, because they could speak their thoughts without restraint.

"I say", said Bob at length, "how far is it to Liverpool, Hiram? Would you say it's further than from Saxmundham to Ipswich?"

"I couldn't tell you", said Hiram, "but I doubt it is."

"Then it must be a terrible long way to Canada", said Bob.

"Ay", said Hiram, with a stoical grin. "I wonder where we shall sleep tonight?"

"I wonder", said Bob, thoughtfully filling his pipe.

They had never spent a night away from home in their lives.

"I say", said Hiram suddenly, "I wonder what'll become of those two teams of ourn. Best horses in the parish those."

"They'll have to get hired men", replied Bob, "unless Harry and Ern give up the stock: but they aren't much good with the plough."

"No, that they aren't", said Hiram gloomily. "I hope whoever get 'em 'll look after 'em proper. They're rare fine horses, they are, to plough."

"That's the truth", said Bob. "But you know, Hiram, hired men 'on't work like we used to. There's a lot in using a plough, isn't there Hiram?"

"Yes", said Hiram stolidly, "there is."

"You've got to know how to set your hake", Bob continued earnestly, as if he were giving Hiram a lesson, "and your share and your coulter, and how to keep your furrow straight. I wonder if they'll be able to do all that."

Hiram sighed.

"Yes", he said, "that summerland of ourn look a treat, don't it, so neat and reg'lar all over; and those clover ricks you and me built last summer – as trim as beehives, aren't they, Bob?"

"Yes, it's a tidy little farm and no mistake", said Bob once more.

"It'd be a pity if that went down like after we'd gone", said Hiram with another sigh.

"That it would", said Bob, "and I don't know as there's a man in the parish fit to work on that farm."

"No, nor do I", replied Hiram.

They sat and smoked in silence for a while. All their interest in the fields that flew past them had faded: they were both thinking of Crakenhill. Suddenly Bob looked up.

"I say", he said impulsively, "let's go back, Hiram."

Hiram nodded.

"P'r'aps it'd be better", he replied.

H. W. Freeman, *Joseph and His Brethren*

7. ENVOI

On the other hand, if memory creates no illusion, and the name of a certain place is associated with one of the golden moments of life, it were rash to hope that another visit would repeat the experience of a bygone day. For it was not merely the sights that one beheld which were the cause of joy and peace; however lovely the spot, however gracious the sky, these things external would not have availed, but for contributory movements of mind and heart and blood, the essentials of the man as then he was. Whilst I was reading this afternoon my thoughts strayed, and I found myself recalling a hillside in Suffolk, where, after a long walk, I rested drowsily one midsummer day twenty years ago. A great longing seized me; I was tempted to set off at once, and find again that spot under the high elm trees, where, as I smoked a delicious pipe, I heard about me the crack, crack, crack of broom-pods bursting in the glorious heat of the noontide sun. Had I acted upon the impulse, what chance was there of my enjoying such another hour as that which my memory cherished? No, no; it is not the *place* that I remember; it is the time of life, the circumstances, the mood, which at that moment fell so happily together. Can I dream that a pipe smoked on that same hillside, under the same glowing sky, would taste as it then did, or bring me the same solace? Would the turf be so soft beneath me? Would the great elm-branches temper so delightfully the noontide rays beating upon them? And, when the hour of rest was over, should I spring to my feet as then I did, eager to put forth my strength again? No, no; what I remember is just one moment of my earlier life, linked by accident with that picture of the Suffolk landscape. The place no longer exists; it never existed save for me. For it is the mind which creates the world about us, and even though we stand side by side in the same meadow, my eyes will never see what is beheld by yours, my heart will never stir to the emotions with which yours is touched.

George Gissing, *The Private Papers of Henry Ryecroft*

Acknowledgements

The author and publishers are grateful to the following for permission to use copyright material:

William Blackwood (*There's Rosemary, There's Rue* by Winifred Fortescue)

Geoffrey Bles (*Happy Countryman* by C. H. Warren)

The Bodley Head Ltd (*Unknown Suffolk* by Donald Maxwell)

Jonathan Cape (*Peter Duck* and *Secret Water* by Arthur Ransome, 'A Note from a Cello' from *Celebrations* by William Plomer)

Chatto and Windus (*Joseph and his Brethren* and *Down the Valley* by H. W. Freeman; *Collected Essays* by Virginia Woolf)

Constable Publishers (*Looming Lights* by George Carter)

Faber and Faber (*Thorofare* by Christopher Morbey; *Suffolk Punch* by George Cross; *Acky* by George Ewart Evans; 'The Other Side of the Alde' by Lord Clark and 'The Suffolk Countryside' by the Earl of Cranbrook, from *A Tribute to Benjamin Britten on his Fiftieth Birthday*, ed. Anthony Gishford; *Britten* by Imogen Holst)

Victor Gollancz (*Bread or Blood* by A. J. Peacock)

Hamish Hamilton ('Feet Foremost' from *The Complete Short Stories of L. P. Hartley*)

The Hamlyn Group (*Reminiscences of Country Life* by James Cornish)

George C. Harrap & Co Ltd (*Harvest Adventure* and *Farming Adventure* by James Wentworth Day)

David Higham Associates (*Akenfield* by Ronald Blythe)

Hutchinson Publishing Group (*The Suffolk Landscape* by Norman Scarfe; *The Cottage in the Forest* by Hugh Farmer; *Corduroy* by Adrian Bell; *Suffolk Childhood* by Simon Dewes)

Allan Jobson (*This Suffolk*)

John Murray ('Felixstowe' from *Collected Poems* by Sir John Betjeman)

Routledge and Kegan Paul (*East Anglian Folklore* by W. H. Barrett and R. P. Garrod)

Secker and Warburg (*Anglo-Saxon Attitudes* by Angus Wilson)

Leonard P. Thompson (*Old Inns of Suffolk*)

While every effort has been made to identify and trace copyright owners, the editor and publishers apologise for any inadvertent omissions.

Index of Authors